Miniatures
and
Morals

To read more about the following titles by
Peter J. Leithart, visit www.canonpress.org

From Silence to Song
The Davidic Liturgical Revolution

Against Christianity

A Son to Me
An Exposition of 1 & 2 Samuel

A House For My Name
A Survey of the Old Testament

Blessed Are the Hungry
Meditations on the Lord's Supper

Heroes of the City of Man
A Christian Guide to Select Ancient Literature

Ascent to Love
A Guide to Dante's Divine Comedy

Brightest Heaven of Invention
A Christian Guide to Six Shakespeare Plays

Wise Words
Family Stories that Bring the Proverbs to Life

MINIATURES
and
MORALS

The Christian Novels of Jane Austen

Peter J. Leithart

CANON
PRESS
MOSCOW, IDAHO

Peter J. Leithart, *Miniatures and Morals: The Christian Novels of Jane Austen*

© 2004 by Peter Leithart
Published by Canon Press, P.O. Box 8741, Moscow, ID 83843
800-488-2034 / www.canonpress.org

04 05 06 07 08 09 10   9 8 7 6 5 4 3 2 1

Printed in the United States of America.

Cover design by Paige Atwood.

Library of Congress Cataloging-in-Publication Data

Leithart, Peter J.
Miniatures and morals : the Christian novels of Jane Austen /
Peter J. Leithart.
     p. cm.
Includes bibliographical references (p.195) and index.
  ISBN 1-59128-015-X (pbk.)
  1. Austen, Jane, 1775-1817—Religion. 2. Christianity and
literature—England—History—19th century. 3. Christian fiction,
English—History and criticism. 4. Christian ethics in literature. 5.
Christian life in literature. I. Title.
PR4038.R4L45 2004
823'.7—dc22
                                        2003023087

To Emma

Who truly "unites some of the best
blessings of existence"

Contents

Acknowledgments

I fell in love with Jane Austen — as a writer, I mean — nearly a decade ago when I read through Pride and Prejudice to my family. As I read after dinner week by week, my audience dwindled, as the children found various excuses to leave the table and never made good on their promises to return. In the end, I think only Woelke, my oldest, heard me out to the very end, no doubt eager even in that preteen stage of life to find out if Elizabeth and Darcy would end up together. I didn't mind in the least. Even if I had been left at the table all by myself, I would have continued reading aloud, chuckling over Mr. Bennet and his "lady," scoffing at Mr. Collins, and enjoying Elizabeth Bennet's fine wit, which, I imagined, perfectly matched her sparkling eyes. By the time I closed the book, I was not quite a Janeite (evidence: I've no idea how to play whist). I was, however, definitely a settled fan.

My delight in Austen's writing has not diminished over the years since, and my appreciation of her skill and wisdom has only increased, largely due to opportunities to lecture on Austen in various settings. I teach on Pride and Prejudice in my literature survey at New St. Andrews College, and am faced every year with the daunting prospect of trying to provide illumination to students — mostly female — who know Austen far better than I. Daunting, but invaluable, since I have learned far more than I realize about Austen from them.

Several years ago, I received even more help by offering an elective course on Austen, in which we (that is, about a dozen women, one male student, a male auditor, and I) worked through all of Austen's finished works. That course particularly gave me a chance to begin developing the interpretations of the novels I offer in this volume.

During the summer of 2001, I was invited to deliver several talks on literature at the Christian Worldview Student Conference in Newport News, Virginia. Thanks to Pastors Byron Snapp and Pete Hurst for inviting me, and to the students, who met all of the speakers with an enthusiasm that, to me at least, was just shy of frightening. It was there that I first attempted, without much success, to lead students in the chant, "Real Men Read Austen." Even enthusiastic students have their limits. I'm still hopeful the chant will catch on.

More recently, Dean Roy Atwood allowed me to deliver a lecture on Mansfield Park at a New St. Andrews disputatio, and almost convinced Doug Wilson to read the book. I included a lecture on Emma during a week-long survey of Western literature at the 2002 New St. Andrews summer school program, and owe thanks to all those who attended that class, which I remember with much affection.

Finally, thanks to Doug Jones for his interest in this project, and for the continuing support of Canon Press for my various books. Jared Miller, who has helped to edit several of my books, also deserves thanks for smoothing out the manuscript and making this a better book than it would have been.

Miniatures and Morals is dedicated to my second daughter, Emma, who is not named for Emma Woodhouse. In fact, she is nothing like Emma Woodhouse. She would not like Mrs. Elton any more than Emma Woodhouse does, but she would not make fun of her, and my Emma would never, ever say a nasty word to a Miss Bates or have to endure a stinging rebuke from Mr. Knightley. If there is an Austen character she resembles, it is Anne Elliot, or perhaps Fanny Price — quite and slightly shy, compassionate, useful.

Emma is too young to remember my reading Pride and Prejudice to the family and has not yet begun to read Austen herself.

But I trust that, in time, she will find as much delight and instruction in Austen as her father has, and that, reading about her namesake, she will learn compassion, charity, and the discernment to distinguish between a Frank Churchill and a George Knightley.

Peniel Hall
Trinity Season, 2003

CHAPTER 1

Real Men Read Austen

If I had the opportunity to have dinner with a dozen of the greatest British and American writers, I would want the seat next to Jane Austen. Dickens would be too busy jumping up from the table making toasts or serving wine to engage in any real conversation, and I suspect Shakespeare would be much the same (actors always are). Faulkner would be drunk, and Joyce too. Jane—we'd all call her Jane—would not be a wallflower, but she would spend much of her time observing, and another proportion of her time whispering her observations with sometimes mordant sarcasm. Others at the table might *know* more, but Austen would be far and away the most *intelligent* among them.

And the funniest—Dickens' humor would be cartoonish and he would spend the evening doing wildly exaggerated impersonations; Shakespeare's funniest moments would be tinged with slapstick farce, and he would try to one-up Dickens with snippets of Falstaff and a comic Hamlet (actors always do). At a dinner party, though, where wit and irony rather than pratfalls were the source for humor, Jane would excel.

Jane Austen has never been more popular. Several years ago, James Wood wrote a piece in *The New Republic* that was summarized on the cover as "Austen Rules." And indeed she does: her books continue to be widely read; in recent years, several have been made into popular films of varying degrees of faithfulness to the originals; and even the films that bear the titles of the novels do not represent the extent of her influence on movies. *Clueless* is a California-based remake of *Emma*, and *Bridget Jones' Diary* barely conceals its plagiarism of *Pride and Prejudice*. Whit Stillman's trilogy of *Metropolitan, Last Days of Disco*, and *Barcelona* are less obviously drawn from Austen, but all have an Austen-like interest in class and manners, and the first is a modernized *Mansfield Park* with a "truth-telling" game filling the role of the theatrical production in the novel.

Despite her popularity, Austen is often misunderstood—especially by men. When I told friends I was working on a book on Austen, more than one asked, "Why?" and one did not believe me at first. (Note well: no women asked this question.) For many Austen is all tea parties and balls and bonnets, hoop skirts and sentimentality, and her popularity is merely a sign of the craven nostalgia that characterizes much of our early twenty-first century culture, the absurd wish for the simplicity of yesteryear.

Admittedly, there appears to be some ground for this assessment of Austen. Though living through a period that witnessed the birth of an independent United States, the French Revolution and the Terror, the Napoleonic wars and the rise of revolutionary romanticism, the evangelical revivals and the upheavals of the Industrial Revolution, she focuses on a few middling gentry families in rural England. Touches of the wider world sometimes impinge on Austen's peaceful outposts—Wickham, a soldier, plays a prominent role in *Pride and Prejudice*, there are passing references to the British colonies and the slave trade in *Mansfield Park*, and the British navy's preservation of England is duly noted in *Persuasion*. For the most part, her characters go about their farming and their business, their follies and their romances, their dances and their games of backgammon and whist, as if nothing has changed. Soldiers and sailors, when they appear, are always on leave.

Well-read as she and her family were, it is impossible that Austen was ignorant of the transformations taking place around her. She read poetry and novels, including those from the romantic period, and she knew the literature of her time well enough to parody it. We know too that her family was directly affected by a number of these events. Two of her brothers fought Napoleon as members of the British navy. Philadelphia Austen, Jane's aunt, had a daughter named Eliza who married a Frenchman, Jean Capot, Comte de Feuillide. The unfortunate Capot was guillotined during the terror, and his widow Eliza later married Jane's brother Henry to become Jane's sister-in-law. Her favorite brother, Henry, was a clergyman of evangelical stripe, and several letters show that Jane herself knew something of evangelicalism (though she did not like it much). Jane herself toyed with the idea of writing a biography of Napoleon.

How, then, does one account for the almost total absence of the contemporary world in her novels? When this question is raised, many attempt to explain Austen as a purveyor of nostalgia: with her world in upheaval, with everything turning upside down, she retreated into a bunker to fight a rearguard action against the spirit of the age and to offer quaint glimpses of a simpler, happier, saner time and place. Like Mr. Woodhouse in *Emma*, she found change so disagreeable that she chose to pretend it had not happened.

Though Austen's twentieth-century readers (and, even more, viewers) may feel a twinge for a lost world, Austen herself betrays no such sentiment. It is difficult to imagine a less nostalgic writer than Austen; she was too sharp-witted, too much the satirist of manners, and too ironic for that. Her world amused her, but she was keenly aware of the pettiness of many of its inhabitants and she did not shrink from showing their true colors. If you want to get a sense of Austen's *un*sentimentality, you can do this experiment: read *any* Dickens novel (actually, a few pages or chapters would do), then read *any* Austen novel. Ask yourself which is more sentimental. The answer will be obvious.

More credibly, it has been suggested that Austen consciously chose to limit the scope of her concerns for artistic reasons. Charlotte Brontë, though no great admirer of Austen's work, still displayed considerable insight into the kind of writer Austen was. Of *Pride and Prejudice*, Brontë wrote that it was "An accurate daguerreotype portrait of a commonplace face. A carefully fenced, highly cultivated garden, with neat borders and delicate flowers, but no glance of a bright, vivid physiognomy, no open country, no fresh air, no blue hill, no bonny neck." After reading *Emma*, Brontë wrote, "She does her business of delineating the surface of the lives of genteel English people curiously well. There is a Chinese fidelity, a miniature delicacy in the painting."

"Miniature delicacy" captures an important aspect of Austen. But it must be seen as a deliberate limitation, as some of her letters show. Her niece Anna sent her a manuscript of a book she was writing asking for comments, and in a famous reply, Austen writes: "You are now collecting your people delightfully, getting them exactly into such a spot as is the delight of my life. Three or four families in a Country Village is the very thing to work on." In another letter, she advises Anna to stick with things she knows: "we think you [i.e., Anna's characters] had better not leave England. Let the Portmans go to Ireland, but as you know nothing of manners there, you had better not go with them. You will be in danger of giving false representations." When Rev. James Stanier Clarke wrote on behalf of the Prince Regent to thank Austen for a copy of *Emma*, which had been dedicated to the Prince Regent, Clarke suggested that Austen try to write a romance. Austen insisted she would continue to write "such pictures of domestic Life in Country Villages as I deal in." She continued:

> I could no more write a Romance than an Epic Poem—I could not sit seriously down to write a serious Romance under any other motive than to save my life, and if it were indispensable for me to keep it up and never relax into laughing at myself or other people, I am sure I should be hung before I had finished the first Chapter. No, I must keep to my own style and my own way; and though I may never succeed again in that, I am convinced that I should totally fail in any other.

She is being playful here, but expressing, in her playfulness, a clear consciousness of what she can and cannot do. Having never boarded a slaving ship, Austen refused to attempt writing about one; having never visited the colonies, Austen knew she could not accurately depict their manners; having never experienced epic events, she refused to write an epic; but, having spent much of her life in small country towns, she could write about small country towns with insight. More than a few writers could learn from Austen's humility.

This "miniaturism" is manifest in a number of ways. First, she limits herself with regard to characters. Instead of peopling her books with a cast of thousands, as Dickens would later do, she focuses her entire attention on a small group of characters—on three or four families. For the most part, moreover, all her main characters are from a single sector of English society, the middle gentry classes. Members of the higher nobility sometimes appear, but they are almost never central characters and are often held up for ridicule. *Mansfield Park* depicts life in a noble house, but the central character is Fanny Price, a poor cousin who is living with the Bertrams. The few members of lower classes who appear are also on the margins. In *Emma* Harriet Smith is in love with a farmer, Robert Martin, but though he is the focus of considerable attention, we never hear him speak and he appears mainly in reported conversations of Harriet.

Austen also limits her novels with regard to action and setting. Several years ago, I read a few chapters of a book in the Jane Austen, Detective series, a mystery series in which Austen herself plays the sleuth. I was intrigued by the series for two reasons: I believe that Austen, with her extraordinary control of point of view and information, would have written wonderful detective fiction, and I had been told that the novels were written in the same style as Austen's own. Before the first chapter was done, however, Austen's carriage had turned over in a ditch, and she had fallen headlong with her skirts falling down over her head. I put the book aside, as Austen would say, in disgust, and have made a deliberate effort to forget the author. Whatever the virtues of Jane Austen, Detective, the book had little in common with Austen's fiction. Overturned carriages, not to mention overturned heroines, have no place in Austen's world.

In Austen's own novels, it is often said, nothing happens. That is true if one expects carriages to overturn, car chases, or explosions. There is remarkably little violence or vigorous action in Austen's novels. At worst, a Marianne Dashwood falls and sprains her ankle on a hill and later catches a bad cold, or a Louisa Musgrove falls off a wall and receives a nasty bump on the head. One critic said that the most violent thing that happens in *Pride and Prejudice* occurs when Elizabeth jumps over a stile on the way to visit her sick sister. Colonel Brandon and Willoughby fight a duel (neither is wounded), but it is not shown and it is spoken of so cryptically and briefly that readers can easily miss it. Nobody, so far as I can recall, ever *bleeds* in an Austen novel. The settings of Austen's novels are mainly domestic and social, and men never, ever appear except in the company of women. It is definitely a woman's world. Again, the limitation is deliberate; having never entered a smoking room to discuss the day's hunt, Austen does not attempt to depict a fictional smoking room.

This is truly a limitation. Life does include moments of violence and physical peril, and their absence in Austen is one of the main things that makes the novels unappealing to men. Strikingly, too, though her novels are all romances, sex is quite absent and in many respects so is the body. One scholar wrote a monograph on the body in Austen, emphasizing Austen's frequent references to the "fine figures" of both men and women and other references to body parts; but "figure" is a geometric not an anatomical term and seems to reduce the person to a silhouette. Austen's characters have "eyes" and "figures" and sometimes "teeth," but we rarely get an image of a whole body. In terms of personality, Austen's characters are psychologically quite round, but physically they are flat. Novels without sex, violence, and bodies have a feeling of abstraction, something, perhaps, like Auden's "a million eyes, a million boots in line."

Still, I insist that "real men read Austen" and can read her with interest and profit. Austen, after all, created some very striking male characters. Some of her heroes are more than a little effeminate; Edward Ferrars in *Sense and Sensibility* is painfully silent in much of the book, though that is in part due to a depression caused by his secret engagement to the manipulative Lucy Steele, which is plenty to take the pluck out of any man. Henry Tilney in *Northanger Abbey* knows more about fabrics than most men have cause to know. Austen's other heroes, however, are strong and forceful personalities, and definitely *not* effeminate. All her great heroes—Darcy, Wentworth, Edmund Bertram, Knightley—are men who hold positions of authority and use those positions for good. Each of them is a Christlike lover who sacrifices, often at some cost to his reputation, to win his bride. They are servant-heroes, not macho-heroes. For Austen, machismo is just Spanish for "bluster" and is the mark of villainy.

Even without considering her strong male characters, Austen's novels are highly instructive for men. The mere fact that her novels give men an opportunity to see romance through the eyes of an uncommonly perceptive woman should be enough to recommend them. Even if we men do not want to see courtship through a woman's eyes, who can say we do not need to? She has a strong sense of a man's role in courtship and his responsibility for the course that a courtship takes. More than one male character in her novels proves himself a scoundrel by playing with the affections of a woman. Austen's first rule of courtship is one I have frequently repeated to my sons: Men are responsible not only for behaving honorably toward women but also for the woman's response; if a man does not intend to enter a serious relationship, he has no business giving a woman special attention or encouraging her to attach herself to him. Austen sees clearly that men who play with a woman's affections are fundamentally egotistical. They want the admiration and attention of women without promising anything or making any commitment. Few lessons of courtship are more needed in our own day.

In fact, even the apparent lack of incident in Austen's novels is part of their particular strength. The events of an Austen novel are the kinds of incidents that most people are involved in most days and weeks and months of their lives. Nothing happens in Austen— nothing but marriages, engagements entered into and broken, scandals exposed, evenings spent in conversation at the card table or around the fire, secrets kept and revealed, promises made and kept or broken. If "nothing happens" in Austen, it is because "nothing happens" most of the time. Yet, precisely because of this limitation, because so little seems to happen, every nuance and contour of what *does* happen takes on considerable importance. We begin to realize that men can be cads without kidnaping women and confining them in dark towers, and women can be vicious without poisoning their rivals. Men can be cads just by being male (John Thorpe in *Northanger Abbey* is the prime illustration), and women can kill as effectively with words as with arsenic. If we read Austen sensitively and begin to see things through her eyes, we begin to realize that much is happening in our lives even, or especially, at those frequent moments when "nothing is happening." If this is a "feminine" vision of the world, it is one that men would do well to pay attention to. For it is not good that we should be alone.

Austen's style is consistent with her limitation of character, setting, and plot. She is a miniaturist in style, in that she does more with less than any other writer in English. There is a precision and lack of ornamentation in her prose that I suspect owes much to the Bible and the Prayer Book. This makes her simply the best prose stylist, and one of the most innovative, in English literature (Shakespeare is better, but wrote mostly poetry). After reading Austen, every other writer's style seems bloated, even—dare I blaspheme—as elegant a stylist as C. S. Lewis. Several examples will help to make the point.

One dimension of this economy is that she pays her readers the compliment of not spelling out everything explicitly. She expects her readers to be intelligent enough to draw conclusions from the information she gives. Toward the end of *Pride and Prejudice*, Lady Catherine de Bourgh shows up at Longbourn in an attempt to pressure Elizabeth Bennet to give up all hopes of marrying Darcy. During this remarkably spirited exchange, Lady Catherine reveals that she received a report about the engagement "two days ago." On the preceding page, in a conversation with Mrs. Bennet,

she said that she had left the Collinses well "the night before last."
In this case, the conclusion is drawn later by Elizabeth when she
realizes that Lady Catherine had heard the rumor of Darcy's im-
pending engagement from the Collinses. But we were given all
the facts we needed from Lady Catherine herself, and we as well as
Elizabeth could have put two and two together. Similarly, at several points in *Emma*, Miss Bates provides crucial information about
Frank Churchill and Jane Fairfax, but we need to pay careful attention to her rambling speeches to get the point. At the end of
Emma, Mrs. Elton complains about the lack of elegance at Emma's
wedding, but the narrator subtly informs us that she was not in
fact present by saying that she drew her conclusions "from the
particulars detailed by her husband."

Austen also frequently leaves much of a setting and even characters to the imagination. Writing to Anna, she offered this advice: "You describe a sweet place, but your descriptions are often
more minute than will be liked. You give too many particulars of
right hand and left." Austen often creates the illusion of a scene
with only a few strokes, a few props, like a caricaturist who can
capture a face with a few lines. On Knightley's first visit to Hartfield
at the beginning of *Emma*, nothing in the room is mentioned
besides a backgammon table, a fire, and a visitor. There is no
description of Knightley's physical appearance, or of the room,
and even some of the "props" used to set the scene are noted by
the characters rather than by the narrator. Other writers, like
Charlotte Brontë, cannot bear to introduce a character without a
photographic description.

John Reed was a schoolboy of fourteen years old . . . large and
stout for his age, with a dingy and unwholesome skin; thick lin-
eaments in a spacious visage, heavy limbs and large extremities.
He gorged himself habitually at table, which made him bilious,
and gave him a dim and bleared eye and flabby cheeks.
(*Jane Eyre*, chap.1)

A snug, small room; a round table by a cheerful fire; an armchair
high-backed and old-fashioned, wherein sat the neatest imagin-
able elderly lady, in widow's cap, black silk gown and snowy muslin

apron; exactly like what I had fancied Mrs. Fairfax only less stately
and milder looking. She was occupied in knitting: a large cat sat
demurely at her feet; nothing in short was wanting to complete
the beau-ideal of domestic comfort. (*Jane Eyre*, chap. 11)

One of the reasons Austen avoids this kind of detail is that it so
often slips into tired clichés (like "tired cliché," for example). If
there is a fire, then by all means it must be "cheerful"; and I daresay
that every fourteen-year-old boy who has ever appeared in any
novel is either "large" or "small" for his age (whatever happened
to all the average-sized fictional fourteen-year-old boys?). Yet
Austen's economy does not make her characters any less vivid and
alive. Most readers of *Pride and Prejudice* come away feeling they
know Elizabeth and Darcy, though we know very little about their
appearance—height, weight, eye and hair color, stoutness of limbs
and eating habits are left entirely to the imagination. As noted
above, the lack of bodiliness is a problem, but Austen nearly makes
up for it with psychological richness.

Austen not only limits the number of characters but creates
them with an economy that borders on the miraculous. The first
chapter of *Pride and Prejudice* provides a delightful example; after
a little more than two pages of dialogue, we know Mr. and Mrs.
Bennet, their relationship with each other, their relationships with
their daughters, their hopes and dreams, their faults and follies.
The characterization of Mr. Collins is a more complex illustration. Before he appears in *Pride and Prejudice*, he has been introduced by a letter, in which he discusses his breach with the Bennet
family and his eventual inheritance of the Bennet home at
Longbourn:

> The disagreement subsisting between yourself and my later
> honoured father, always gave me much uneasiness, and since I
> have had the misfortune to lose him, I have frequently wished to
> heal the breach; but for some time I was kept back by my own
> doubts, fearing lest it might seem disrespectful to his memory
> for me to be on good terms with anyone, with whom it
> had always pleased him to be at variance. . . . As a clergyman,

moreover, I feel it my duty to promote and establish the blessing of peace in all families within the reach of my influence; and on these grounds I flatter myself that my present overtures of good-will are highly commendable, and that the circumstance of my being next in the entail of Longbourn estate, will be kindly over-looked on your side, and not lead you to reject the olive branch.

This passage illustrates a central tenet of Austen's writing—namely, that syntax is character. *How* someone speaks manifests the quality of his mind and character as much as or even more than *what* he says. Anyone who writes and speaks with a style as convoluted and orotund as Collins cannot be sensible. Elizabeth gets him exactly right: "There is something pompous in his style," and if style is pompous, so is the man.

Lydia Bennet provides another example. Ignoring Elizabeth's protests, she describes her wedding to Wickham: "We were married, you know, at St. Clement's, because Wickham's lodgings were in that parish. And it was settled that we should all go there by eleven o'clock. My uncle and aunt and I were to go together; and the others were to meet us at the church. . . . And so we break-fasted at ten as usual. . . ." Yada, yada, yada. Like her sentences, Lydia's life is just one breathless thing after another. Elizabeth is right to wonder how a young woman who speaks this way can hope to find a shred of permanent happiness in marriage.

One of my favorite examples is from *Emma*, where Austen relates Mrs. Elton's stream of consciousness during a strawberry picking outing at Knightley's Donwell Abbey:

The best fruit in England—everybody's favourite—always whole-some. These the finest beds and finest sorts. Delightful to gather for oneself—the only way of really enjoying them. Morning decidedly the best time—never tired—every sort good—hautboy infinitely superior—no comparison—the others hardly eatable—hautboys very scarce—Chili preferred—white wood finest flavour of all—price of strawberries in London—abundance about Bristol—Maple Grove—cultivations—beds when to be renewed—gardeners thinking exactly different—no general rule—

gardeners never to be put out of their way—delicious fruit—
only too rich to be eaten much of—inferior to cherries—cur-
rants more refreshing—only objections to gathering strawberries
the stooping—glaring sun—tire to death—could bear it no
longer—must go and sit in the shade.

Mrs. Elton is all here: the contradictory opinions, each stated
with utter confidence, the randomness, the reversion to obsessive
themes (her home of Maple Grove), the domineering know-it-
allness. One fragmented paragraph captures a whole person.

One indication of Collins' poverty of style, and hence of mind,
is poverty of metaphor. Austen has been characterized as a relent-
lessly non-metaphorical writer, but that is an error. Though she
rarely uses explicit similes ("he is like a beast") or metaphors
(though she did write in a letter, "I am a beast"), her language and
her imagination are metaphorical in a different, and perhaps more
profound, sense. She has an intuitive grasp of the inherent relat-
edness of things, and any careful study of her language will show
that she often adapts language from one realm of life to describe
another (e.g., economic language to describe romance). When
she wishes, she is capable of producing striking metaphorical descriptions: In *Emma* she writes of Mrs. Elton's bonnet and basket
as her "apparatus of happiness"; when she describes the aftermath
of Elton's proposal to Emma by saying that "their straightforward
emotions left no room for the little zig-zags of embarrassment";
and in *Sense and Sensibility*, she refers to the "puppyism" of Robert Ferrars's manners. All of these are very original, funny, and apt
coinages.

What Austen despises is not metaphor, but metaphors that are
so overworked that they ought to have been retired long ago. In a
letter to Anna she warns against using the phrase "vortex of Dissipation" explaining, "I do not object to the thing, but I cannot
bear the expression; it is such thorough novel slang; and so old,
that I dare say Adam met with it in the first novel he opened."
Metaphors tend to die and fossilize, and once this happens they
can be used without thought. Like the orotund style, Collins' use

of the "olive branch" is a sign of his stupidity, for that is a meta-phor as old as Noah, if not Adam.

Austen uses Collins' letter, however, not only to characterize Collins, but to fill in the caricature of the letter's hearers as well. After Mr. Bennet reads the letter, the Bennets react to it. Mrs. Bennet is the first:

> "There is some sense in what he says about the girls . . . and if he is disposed to make them any amends, I shall not be the person to discourage him."
>
> "Though it is difficult," said Jane, "to guess in what way he can mean to make us the atonement he thinks our due, the wish is certainly to his credit."
>
> Elizabeth was chiefly struck with his extraordinary deference for Lady Catherine, and his kind intention of christening, mar-rying, and burying his parishioners whenever it was required.
>
> "He must be an oddity, I think," said she. "I cannot make him out.—There is something very pompous in his stile.—And what can he mean by apologizing for being next in the entail?—We cannot suppose he would help it, if he could.—Can he be a sensible man, sir?"
>
> "No, my dear; I think not [said Mr. Bennet]. I have great hopes of finding him quite the reverse. There is a mixture of servility and self-importance in his letter, which promises well. I am impatient to see him."
>
> "In point of composition," said Mary, "his letter does not seem defective. The idea of the olive branch perhaps is not wholly new, yet I think it is well expressed."
>
> To Catherine and Lydia, neither the letter nor its writer were in any degree interesting. It was next to impossible that their cousin [Mr. Collins] should come in a scarlet coat, and it was now some weeks since they had received pleasure in any other colour.

It is only a single page, but this time Austen has provided insight into not one character, but six: Mrs. Bennet thinks of nothing but her own financial security and that of her daughters; Jane is perceptive, but reluctant to criticize; Elizabeth also recog-nizes the defects in Mr. Collins, but is readier than Jane to form a negative opinion of him; Mary shows herself to be as pompous, self-important, and unthinking as Collins himself; and Catherine and Lydia are heedless of their future security, so long as they continue to meet some soldiers in the street.

Elsewhere, Austen uses other objects or activities as "props" and characterizes people by their use of or reaction to them. Music is a key prop; a character's interest in and appreciation for music is a strong indicator of character. Books are another common prop. Over the course of *Pride and Prejudice*, nearly every character's relation to books is noted, and this provides an important clue to character. Mr. Bennet uses books as a means of escaping from his silly wife; quick and sociable Bingley does not read much; Darcy not only reads widely but has a library that has taken several generations to assemble; Miss Bingley picks up a book only so that Darcy will notice and appreciate her desire to learn; Elizabeth reads, but has many other interests as well. By leaving her world nearly empty of objects, Austen is able to increase the significance of each object that is there. The significance, however, is not in the objects themselves, but in what the objects tell us about the people. Notice too that none of these characters can be developed except by similarity and contrast with other characters. No one is a character in isolation; each has his unique features only by *différance*, if you will, from another character's features.

Behind Austen's aesthetic decision to limit herself to what she knows is a "philosophical" stance that can be described as vaguely nominalist. Particulars, Austen sensed, are all we can talk about with any degree of accuracy; about universals we can say very little that is defined or delineated. Universals, by their very nature, lack particular qualities. In *Northanger Abbey*, Henry Tilney's discourse on the theory of the picturesque ends in silence, but not before a long detour:

> Delighted with [Catherine Morland's] progress, and fearful of wearying her with too much wisdom at once, Henry suffered the subject to decline, and by an easy transition from a piece of rocky

fragment and the withered oak which he had placed near its summit, to oaks in general, to forests, the inclosure of them, wastelands, crown lands and government, he shortly found himself arrived at politics; and from politics, it was an easy step to silence.

The larger the scope of discourse, the less opportunity Austen saw for fine discrimination, for the nuances and shades of difference that are necessary for knowledge. The larger the scope of discourse, the more everything blurs into the undifferentiated "smoothness" that Austen (with many of her characters) abhorred.

Precisely this "nominalism," and minute attention to details of character and relation that accompany it, make Austen's work a continuing source of both delight and moral instruction. *Because* of her limitations, she emphasizes the domestic and local context for moral decisions and action. For Austen, the sensational or extraordinary do not provide a sound basis for moral education and experience. Hers is not a "lifeboat ethics" focusing on the marginal extremes of ethical decisions. On the contrary, she recognizes that the greatest ethical challenges come in the midst of daily life, precisely when "nothing is happening."

We will treat some dimensions of Austen's moral outlook in the next chapter, using *Pride and Prejudice* to illustrate how Austen develops moral themes. A few general points can be made here. Unlike some twentieth-century novelists and philosophers (especially existentialists), Austen's novels do not pose ultimate questions. She does not struggle against a void or probe the ultimate mysteries of the universe. In part this is a heritage of the eighteenth-century reaction against scholasticism in both its medieval Catholic and Protestant forms. In Austen's case, I believe, she does not pose these kinds of questions because for her they are not questions. They are settled; a lifelong member of the Anglican church, she believed that the ultimate questions could be answered by consulting the Thirty-Nine Articles.

For a Christian writer, the real challenge of life is not to puzzle the ultimate realities, but to live well in very particular social and domestic settings. The moral philosopher Alasdair MacIntyre discerns an Aristotelian trait in Austen's recognition that virtues are formed, tested, and manifested within community. As Aristotle pointed out, this makes ethics a subdivision of politics—that is, it makes the question "What should I do?" a sub-question under "What kind of community do I wish to live in, and what is my place in it?"

For both Austen and Aristotle, the ethical life is status-specific. That is, to answer "What should I do in this case?" we must ask, "Who am I?" And this latter question is not a question about some inner ghostly "I," but about the role and status I have in a particular society. Darcy must not only ask, "Shall I, who love Elizabeth Bennet's fine eyes, pursue Elizabeth Bennet?" but "Shall I, with my name and status as an English nobleman, pursue Elizabeth Bennet?" When Knightley castigates Emma for her treatment of Miss Bates, he challenges her on precisely this point: Consider your position in the society of the town, he says, and the obligation that your position places on you to show kindness to an unfortunate (if silly) spinster like Miss Bates. Given the well-defined strata of the communities that Austen deals in, this is a more obvious question for her characters than it might be for us. But it is still a central ethical question. Deciding what is right is never simply a matter of "What should I as a human being do?" but always "What should I as a male high school student, or I as a wife, or I as a car mechanic, do in *this* or *that* situation?" This is not relativism; it does not mean that there are no absolutes of right and wrong. But it does mean that the absolutes have particular applications to particular people in particular circumstances. As a father, it is right for me to spank my children; as children, it is not right for my children to spank me. Only the most sophomoric ethics ignores that moral decisions are specific to circumstances, and Austen was no sophomore.

To put the point another way, Austen's ethical vision emphasizes the fact that we are constantly shaped, limited, and qualified by others around us. Ethics is not just about individuals seeking to live a good life or about solitary decision-making trying to achieve ethical perfection; we are simply not isolated like that. Moral training is in the community, or, as Aristotle said, the ethical life is lived in the *polis*. Living an ethical life necessarily involves living in a community and seeking to benefit that community. Aristotle is not a Christian, but we can find a similar point in the Bible. Jesus gave us two great commandments, the latter of which assumes that our lives are lived in the presence of "neighbors." Most of the fruits of the Spirit are virtues that are evident only in the context of life in the church; the Spirit must give us patience because we are surrounded by exasperating people who try our patience. Hermits have little to challenge their patience.

Since for Austen moral life is lived within a particular form of social life, she is deeply concerned with the issue of moral education and guidance. For a community to pass on its particular moral shape to the next generation, that generation needs to receive training and instruction in the expected virtues of the community. This is the reason for the concentration of ancient writers on matter of education or *paedeia*. For Plato, the manner and content of education largely determines the moral tone of a culture. Austen, concerned with morals within a particular community, is also concerned with what can be called the moral education of her characters. Indeed, this is one of her central themes.

This moral vision is the source of Austen's comedy, in two ways. First, she is a humorist because she is a moralist. Like Elizabeth Bennet, she finds folly enormously diverting and makes it diverting for her readers. But, also like Elizabeth Bennet, she finds folly diverting only because she never mocks what is genuinely good. Her recognition of the gap between the good and the real opens up space for her satire. Second, the complexity of her moral vision prevents her from being a simple moralist, or a simple humorist. If you spot irony in Austen, it is likely that there is at least one further layer to it. Henry Tilney, as we shall see in chapter three, rebukes Catherine Morland for her naive Gothic fantasies, and we all laugh condescendingly at Catherine. But Austen gives the whole scene another twist by showing that Catherine faces evils that are very like those of a Gothic heroine. Austen is capable of these layers of literary irony because she sees the multilayered ironies of real life.

At this point, we may finally fully justify the claim that "real men read Austen." For at this point we can recognize that Austen, who appears so completely indifferent to the swirling world around her, is constantly commenting on and evaluating that world. Her nominalism means that she evaluates the world not by looking at things like "The French Revolution" or "The Napoleonic Wars." Not only did she lack firsthand knowledge of these "events," but for Austen they were so big that anything that might be said about them would be "all smoothness." Instead of a thin description of large events, she gives us a thick description of small events. And in so doing, she is busy evaluating what one Austen scholar calls the "revolution behind the revolutions." Even if this is not her intent, she gives us considerable help in sorting through the cultural revolutions of our own world.

Language and manners are the key points in her evaluation. Austen is not, as noted above, simply concerned with what her characters say; to repeat, syntax is character. But for Austen this is not merely a literary device. It is a moral and political principle. Were Austen living and writing today, she would no doubt be shocked at the smarminess of contemporary public discussion, but she would also recognize a sign of severe cultural ruin in the inability of people (especially young people) to speak two sentences together without a heavy peppering of "you knows," "justs," "likes," or "kewls." Crime statistics would alarm her, but she would have much more to say about our un-code of manners that refuses to recognize hierarchy of any sort, that oscillates between chumminess and rudeness, that insinuates viciousness and dishonesty into everyday social contacts. By focusing our attention on these sorts of cultural *signa*, Austen alerts us to some of the unrecognized habits that make it so exceedingly difficult for us to continue the conversation that is contemporary society.

In this respect, Austen is a far more profound cultural and political commentator than the far more overtly political Dickens. Anyone can discern the evils of the factory system or the Terror.

But it takes considerable wisdom to discern the evils embedded in the staccato blather of a seventeen-year-old girl. And it takes an almost unique genius to notice the inner connection between that blather and the evils of revolutionary politics.

I wish to make one more step in my argument, and this is the riskiest of all. I have contended that Austen is worth reading for the insight she gives us into the predominantly *masculine* world of culture and politics, as well as for the careful treatment of romance and domesticity. But I wish to argue further that she is not merely a public intellectual of considerable importance, but a public *theologian*. I submit that Austen is among the most theologically sophisticated of English novelists. George Eliot actually translated books of theology, but her theological outlook was of the tired, clichéd liberal variety. Dickens' Bible bled over his pages almost as much as Bunyan's, but in the end Dickens is also a liberal sentimentalist, who believes in the innocence of children and the saving power of humanitarian kindness. Defoe is orthodox, but nowhere near so profound a theologian as Austen, and not even in the same category in purely literary terms.

The full development of this conclusion is found scattered throughout my analyses of individual books (but even there I do not make a full case for my claim). Several preliminary points may be made here. First, it is true that explicit theological themes rarely arise in either Austen's novels or letters. She displays an Anglican reticence about religious affections, and an Anglican avoidance of the nicer points of theology. Yet we have sufficient evidence to show that she was an orthodox Christian. She was the daughter of a clergyman, two of her brothers were clergymen, she was baptized into the church of England, and spent her entire life as a member of that church. On her deathbed, her brothers were there to administer communion, and her last words were a request that her sister, Cassandra, pray that she have patience. The inscription on the gravestone in the cathedral where she was buried reads as follows:

In memory of
JANE AUSTEN, youngest daughter of the late Reverend George
Austen, formerly Rector of Steventon. She departed this life on
the 18th July 1817, aged 41, after a long illness supported with
the patience and the hopes of a Christian. The benevolence of
her heart, the sweetness of her temper, and the extraordinary
endowments of her mind obtained the regard of all who knew
her, and the warmest love of her intimate connections. Their
grief is in proportion to their affection they know their loss to be
irreparable, but in the deepest affliction they are consoled by a
firm though humble hope that her charity, devotion, faith and
purity have rendered her soul acceptable in the sight of her
REDEEMER.

This hardly seems an accurate characterization of the writer,
since "sweetness of temper" does not describe the woman who
wrote *Sense and Sensibility*. Yet, there is no reason to doubt that
she really did profess Christian faith. Her brother testified that
her views in religion "accorded strictly with those of our Established Church."

Austen shows little interest in speculative theology, or in religious experience. Still, her novels, like all comedies, may be read
as allegories of redemption. The moral insight achieved by her
flawed heroines often looks like a religious conversion, and even
the sudden surprise of love pierces like an arrow of grace. Her
men are hardly perfect, but they frequently "save" the heroines,
often from the rakish "serpents" who would seduce them. Just as
often the bride "saves" the flawed hero. In either case, salvation
comes so that man and wife can come together in the consummation of a marriage. Harold Bloom has characterized Austen's novels as Protestant:

> C. S. Lewis, who read Milton as though the fiercest of Protestant
> temperaments had been an orthodox Anglican, also seems to have
> read Jane Austen by listening for her echoings of the New Testa-
> ment. Quite explicitly, Lewis named Austen as the daughter of

Dr. Samuel Johnson, greatest of literary critics and rigorous Christian moralist:

> I feel . . . sure that she is the daughter of Dr. Johnson: she inherits his common sense, his morality, even much of his style. . . .

That Jane Austen is a wise writer is indisputable, but we do not read *Pride and Prejudice* as though it were Ecclesiastes. Doubtless, Austen's religious ideas were as profound as Samuel Richardson's were shallow, but *Emma* and [Richardson's] *Clarissa* are Protestant novels without being in any way religious.

What most interests Austen about Christianity, however, is its public and institutional dimension, its role as a national "teacher" of morals. Hence her recurring interest in the clergy. Two of her clerical characters, Collins and Elton, are morons; she has no tolerance for this kind of religious pretension and hypocrisy. Nor does she have much use for the vacuous religiosity of Dr. Grant in *Mansfield Park*, who is a pastor only in name and not in fact. This hardly means that she is anticlerical; some of the most severe satire of the clergy in church history has come from devout Christians incensed at the abuses of their leaders. Like them, Austen attacks false clergy not to destroy clergy; she attacks false clergy to defend the true.

On the other side, several of her heroes are ordained or soon to be so. Edward Ferrars is a nonentity in this regard, and one fears that Henry Tilney is too detached and ironic to be much of a pastor, though he provides both intellectual and moral training for Catherine Morland. Still the fact is that in half of Austen's novels the hero is a clergyman. The last of the clerical heroes, Edmund Bertram, is far and away the best model, and the issue of the public role of the church takes on a great deal of importance in *Mansfield Park*. (Here I must reveal that I consider *Mansfield Park* her greatest novel, if not the most fun to read.) Edmund is speaking for the author when he defends the necessity of the pastoral office in response to the laughing, seductive secularism of Mary Crawford. Not only in preaching and teaching, but in life and character, a minister must give himself to the flock: If "a clergyman does not live among his parishioners and prove himself by constant attention their well-wisher and friend, he does very little either for their good or for his own." But if he does live and teach among his parishioners, the manners of the nation are improved even if they do not become more "polished."

Once the fact of Austen's recurring interest in the institutions of the church is noted, other aspects of her novels can be seen to contribute to a deeply Christian vision of community life. In a sense, her theological interests are as ecclesiological as George Eliot's, though she was not self-consciously anthropological as Eliot was. In any case, we can examine the novels as to the contribution they make to this vision. In the next chapter, I examine some of the main themes of Austen's books, using *Pride and Prejudice*. After that, I analyze the novels in chronological order of their composition. *Northanger Abbey* explores the role of imagination and imaginative literature in the moral life, and in a climactic scene points to the evils that plague a "Christian" people like the English. *Sense and Sensibility* examines the requirement of self-restraint, and the painful results of the secrecy that is inherent in social life. *Mansfield Park* has already been mentioned as Austen's most explicitly theological novel, and *Emma* is as fully Christian if less overt, since it concerns charity, especially as exercised in a small town and among close friends. Finally, in the background of *Persuasion* is a sociological contrast between the self-absorbed but increasingly useless nobility and the self-sacrificing heroism of the British navy. Though theological themes are not always openly examined, and though other issues dominate the surface of Austen's novels, I believe that a case can be made for reading her as a public theologian. This may not be the most important way to read Austen, but it is one that highlights important dimensions of her impressive works.

And so I return to my dinner party, more certain than ever that I want the seat next to Jane, confident now that I would relish not only the entertainment of the evening, but that I would return home quite edified.

CHAPTER 2

Morals and Manners, Marriage and Money:
Pride and Prejudice

Jane Austen's novels are repetitive both in plot and theme. Every novel is a romance and a comedy and each follows a standard pattern: A young man and a young woman are introduced, and normally there is an immediate attraction between them. Obstacles arise, however, that keep the two lovers from declarations of love, engagement, and marriage. Usually one obstacle is the presence of a rival lover who vies with the male hero for the love of his lady. Late in the book the rival lover is exposed as a villain of one degree or another; a shady past finally catches up with him or he runs off with someone more elegant, more lively, or more wealthy. Once the rival lover is out of the way, the hero and heroine are free to finish off what was started at the beginning. Like all romantic comedies, Austen's books invariably end in marriage. At times, the plots are made more complex by a secondary romance that runs parallel to the primary one.

Anyone with minimal knowledge of the novels can fill in the blanks. In the column for "romantic heroine," put Elizabeth (and Jane) Bennet, Catherine Morland, Elinor (and Marianne) Dashwood, Fanny Price, Emma Woodhouse, and Anne Elliot. Fill in the blanks for "romantic hero" with Darcy (and Bingley), Henry Tilney, Edward Ferrars (and Colonel Brandon), Edmund Bertram, Mr. Knightley, and Captain Wentworth. The villains are Wickham (and Lady Catherine de Bourgh), John Thorpe, Willoughby (and Mrs. Ferrars), Henry Crawford, Frank Churchill, and William Elliot. There are sometimes interesting variations on the pattern, of course. In *Sense and Sensibility*, for example, the male villain, Willoughby, is not a rival for Elinor's love but for Marianne's, even though Elinor is the central character. Elinor's love for Edward is blocked instead by *female* villains, Edward's mean-spirited mother and Lucy Steele, whose decision to abandon Edward when he is disinherited proves her to be a female version of Willoughby, equally ambitious but infinitely cattier. And the characters in each novel are vivid, unique, and alive. John Thorpe is hardly interchangeable with Henry Crawford, and Fanny Price is no Elizabeth Bennet. Still, the novels are recognizably a set of variations on a single plot.

Thematically as well, Austen is obsessed by a set of recurring issues which can be summarized under the "four *M*s" given in the title of this chapter. Some of these themes are inherent in the type of literature that Austen chose to write. As romantic comedies, the novels are necessarily concerned with marriage, and in Austen's world marital concerns are inseparable from the monetary ones— concerns of property, status, wealth. Given the social world of Austen's novels, moreover, the question of proper and improper manners is bound to be a central concern. Her interest in morals is not so necessary to the form, though most writers of romance in the eighteenth and nineteenth centuries wrote from some moral perspective. Even Henry Fielding, despite the rakishness of his heroes, is *not* the exception that proves the rule, for his stories are in the end expansions of the parable of the Prodigal Son.

I have no complaint against Austen's repetitiveness. She knew what she was about and deals with a remarkable variety of characters and issues within her deliberately limited scope. Still the limits of her plots and central concerns present challenges for a writer on Austen. A chapter on "The Romance of Elizabeth and Darcy" could be followed by a chapter on "The Romance of Elinor and Edward," but they would be in large measure the *same* chapter. Or, a chapter on "The Four *M*s in *Pride and Prejudice*" could be followed by a chapter on "The Four *M*s in *Sense and Sensibility*," but that would be tedious in the extreme, both to write and to read. More seriously, that kind of approach would obscure the unique dimensions of each book—and there *are* unique dimensions.

Instead of writing the same chapter six times, I have chosen to illustrate the major thematic issues in Austen's work in this opening chapter, using *Pride and Prejudice* as the basis for discussion. This novel serves the purpose well, for several reasons. It explicitly deals with each of the four *M*s in a way that will illuminate the rest of the novels and relieve me of the duty of continually returning to the same points. Also, given the popularity of both the book and the film, there is little need to rehearse the story or to examine the characters in detail. This makes it possible to move, without further introduction, to the four *M*s.

Morals

Jane Austen was a moralist, but she clearly believed there are wrong ways to be a moralist. Mary Bennet is the most explicit moralist of *Pride and Prejudice*, but fails miserably in that capacity. Consider this early exchange among Charlotte Lucas, Elizabeth Bennet, and Mary Bennet, concerning Darcy's pride:

> "His pride," said Miss Lucas, "does not offend *me* so much as pride often does, because there is an excuse for it. One cannot wonder that so very fine a young man, with family, fortune, every thing in his favour, should think highly of himself. If I may so express it, he has a *right* to be proud."
>
> "That is very true," replied Elizabeth, "and I could easily forgive *his* pride, if he had not so mortified *mine*."
>
> "Pride," observed Mary, who piqued herself upon the solidity of her reflections, "is a very common failing I believe. By all that I have ever read, I am convinced that it is very common indeed, that human nature is particularly prone to it, and that there are very few of us who do not cherish a feeling of self-complacency on the score of some quality or other, real or imaginary. Vanity and pride are different things, though the words are often used synonymously. A person may be proud without being vain. Pride

relates more to our opinion of ourselves, vanity to what we would have others think of us."

"If I were as rich as Mr. Darcy," cried a young Lucas who came with his sisters, "I should not care how proud I was. I would keep a pack of foxhounds, and drink a bottle of wine every day." (pp. 12–13)[†]

Several features of Mary's moral contribution are significant. Her style is bookish and abstract rather than particular and earthbound. By her own profession she derives most of her insight, such as it is, from books rather than from life. Further, she repeats the same thing again and again, and the point she repeats so emphatically is trite. She is saying only that "pride is common" but she takes a paragraph of several sentences to get it out. As always in Austen, syntax is character, and a character who cannot put thoughts concisely cannot think. Perhaps most importantly, her evaluation of pride is completely ignored by the other characters. The only response she gets is from a child.

Mary's attempts to contribute moral insight are almost always ill-timed. When news of Lydia's elopement with Wickham becomes public, Mary reflects on the consequences of the scandal:

> "This is a most unfortunate affair; and will probably be much talked of. But we must stem the tide of malice, and pour into the wounded bosoms of each other, the balm of sisterly consolation."
>
> Then, perceiving in Elizabeth no inclination of replying, she added, "Unhappy as the event must be for Lydia, we may draw from it this useful lesson; the loss of virtue in a female is irretrievable—that one false step involves her in endless ruin—that her reputation is no less brittle than it is beautiful,—and that she cannot be too much guarded in her behaviour towards the undeserving of the other sex." (p. 198)

Austen is not favorable to any character who employs tattered metaphors like "balm of sisterly consolation." What is most appalling here, however, is Mary's indifference to the actual, real-life

---

[†] All page numbers are from the Norton Critical Edition (YEAR/ED), edited by Donald J. Gray.

pain that Lydia's behavior has caused her family. Her only interest, whether she is reading a book or evaluating another person's conduct, is to make "moral extractions." She has little interest in or capacity for moral *living*.

One of the weaknesses of Mary's bookish moral vision is that it cannot deal with the complexities of life, particularly with the complex problem of moral counterfeits—people who seem moral but are not. In *Pride and Prejudice*, as in all her novels, Austen is preoccupied with the issue of counterfeits of virtue. Collins, for instance, rightly recognizes that his status as a clergyman should shape his decisions, actions, and tastes. He is right to raise such questions as "Is music compatible with the moral life?" But Collins is so overly self-conscious about his position that he caricatures this necessary element of the moral life, and ends up simply pompous and self-absorbed. Instead of really living out his role, he tires to paint the moral life by numbers. Clergymen, he believes, should read only serious books; and so he pretends to read serious books, though he spends most of his time chatting with Mr. Bennet.

Paradoxically, his self-consciousness about his role ends up detaching him from his role; rather than embodying clerical life, living it out from within as it were, he is constantly checking himself against a clerical standard that lies outside. Austen's satire of Collins reveals one important feature of her public theology, for in this novel the representative of the church fulfills no function other than to bow obsequiously before Lady Catherine. Instead of being a shaper and teacher of conduct, as *Mansfield Park*'s Edmund Bertram says pastors should be, Collins' conduct does nothing more than flatter the powers that be. This alliance of the church with power is not only repulsive; it is the source of not a little confusion and pain in the novel.

Wickham is a different kind of counterfeit, presenting a false version of the specific virtue of amiability. In its pure form, "amiability" is a genuine regard for other people. Bingley is amiable in the most perfect sense, warm and friendly to everyone; Jane is another example of true amiability, especially in her determination to evaluate everyone as charitably as possible (Austen calls this disposition "candor"). Wickham is "agreeable," but not genuinely "amiable."

More centrally, *Pride and Prejudice* manifests a moral concern by exploring the two ideas of its title, so that the story can be seen as a moral "allegory" of these two failings. Essentially, pride and prejudice are both moral flaws, as the early conversation of Darcy and Elizabeth on these themes makes clear. Darcy has observed that even the "wisest and best" can be made to seem "ridiculous" by people "whose first object in life is a joke." Elizabeth replies:

> "I hope I am not one of *them*. I hope I never ridicule what is wise or good. Follies and nonsense, whims and inconsistencies *do* divert me, I own, and I laugh at them whenever I can.—But these, I suppose, are precisely what you are without."
>
> "Perhaps that is not possible for any one. But it has been the study of my life to avoid those weaknesses which often expose a strong understanding to ridicule."
>
> "Such as vanity and pride."
>
> "Yes, vanity is a weakness indeed. But pride—where there is a real superiority of mind, pride will always be under good regulation."
>
> Elizabeth turned away to hide a smile. (p. 39)

The dialogue ends with Elizabeth's charge that Darcy's defect is "a propensity to hate everybody," while Darcy claims Elizabeth's flaw is "wilfully to misunderstand them" (p. 40). Though playful in tone, the dialogue establishes the failings of the two principal characters. Darcy "represents" pride; Elizabeth, prejudice.

The moral status of Darcy and Elizabeth are further clarified by contrast with other characters. Both Darcy and Elizabeth have as their closest confidants people who are temperamentally opposite. Jane is inclined to believe everything and think good of everyone, and her "candor" makes Elizabeth's suspicion and prejudice stand out in higher relief. Bingley is genuinely amiable to everyone, easy to talk to, solicitous of everyone's comfort, but Darcy is reserved and unapproachable. These contrasts enable us to see more precisely what is involved in each flaw, at least initially. What does pride look like? Whatever it is, it is not Bingley.

Darcy and Bingley are foils for one another, but also each has his own foil: Darcy is proudly conscious of his position, and Collins is a comic, parodic extreme of this kind of pride. Bingley is genuinely amiable, and his amiability is developed partly in contrast to Wickham's counterfeit of amiability. These minor characters have important roles in the plot, but they also give further definition to the moral issues.

Even this scheme is too simple for Austen, who understands the complexities of moral issues because she understands the complexities of life. In part, this is done by showing that "pride" and "prejudice" are more varied and multidimensional than is apparent on the surface. Even Bingley is accused of a kind of pride during a discussion of his haste in writing. Pride is not just one thing that always takes the same form; instead, there are many shades and colorations of pride. Moreover, pride and prejudice are not sharply distinct issues. Elizabeth comes to see that, in her prejudice against Darcy, she has been proud, and Darcy's pride makes him prejudiced, particularly against the Bennet family. Darcy and Elizabeth are even guilty of the same flaws: Darcy's pride is shown in the fact that once his good opinion is lost, it is lost forever. Elizabeth believes this a failing indeed, but this is precisely what she has with respect to Darcy: She gave up any good opinion of him at their first meeting and does not revise it for some time. This has serious consequences because her confirmed and prideful prejudice makes her ready to accept uncritically everything that Wickham says about Darcy.

Pride can even be something admirable. Darcy's pride is a slightly twisted version of something that is essential to moral life, namely, a sense of position within a community. As noted above, Darcy defends pride: "where there is a real superiority of mind, pride will be always under good regulation." Elizabeth smiles at this, but she essentially agrees that there is such a thing as "proper pride." Eventually, Elizabeth comes to opinion that Darcy has no "improper pride." It would be a moral failing if Darcy did *not* take pride in his position, if he did not accept the responsibilities, the decorum, and the dignity that go with it.

Darcy says early on, "There is in every disposition a tendency to some particular evil, a natural defect, which not even the best education can overcome." Addressing one's moral failings is difficult because we often do not know ourselves very well. As a moral tale, *Pride and Prejudice* is also a story of moral education, and this education is largely an education in self-knowledge. Seeing yourself correctly is the beginning of overcoming your "tendency to some particular evil." Again, the fact that Collins, the representative of the church, has no self-understanding makes it impossible for him to lead others to self-knowledge.

Both of the main characters are guilty of self-deceit and blindness, and their blindness is not limited to moral questions. While visiting the Collinses, Elizabeth keeps bumping into Darcy on her walks, but she does not take the hint that Darcy *intends* "accidentally" to meet her in the garden. At the same time, Darcy is thinking that Elizabeth *must* be falling in love with him and considering what a prize he would be. They continually misjudge each other because, more fundamentally, they have misjudged themselves. Beneath the superficial wittiness and repartee are their very different and radically mistaken interpretations of each other. Elizabeth's moment of self-knowledge comes after Darcy's letter, when she begins to see her own pride. Likewise, stung by Elizabeth's rejection of his proposal, Darcy renounces his pride. By confronting error, Darcy saves Elizabeth from damning self-delusion, and by condemning his pride Elizabeth becomes Darcy's "savior." Both see themselves clearly for the first time and convert.

Significantly for both Elizabeth and Darcy the one who challenges and wounds is the savior and the best lover. Not everyone in the novel sees this truth. Miss Bingley thinks she can gain Darcy's affections by never crossing or disagreeing with him, much as Collins thinks he honors Lady Catherine by his irritating deference. For a wise, insightful person, however, those who challenge, provoke, and attack are most attractive and interesting. Elizabeth concludes that this was the reason Darcy fell in love with her:

The fact is, that you were sick of civility, of deference, of officious attention. You were disgusted with the women who were
always speaking and looking, and thinking for *your* approbation
alone. I roused, and interested you, because I was so unlike *them*.
Had you not been really amiable, you would have hated me for
it; but in spite of the pains you took to disguise yourself, your
feelings were always noble and just; and in your heart, you thoroughly despised the persons who so assiduously courted you
(p. 262).

The one who makes sure you do *not* get your way is your best
friend. Few services are more useful, Austen believes, than notic-
ing and correcting the errors of others, and this is one of many
indications of Austen's belief that the moral life cannot be lived in
isolation, but only *together.*

Though Austen's novel is not straightforward social commentary, both Darcy and Elizabeth manifest the moral defects of a
particular social class. Darcy's pride, both proper and improper, is
an aspect of his noble standing, while Elizabeth's prejudice is partly
a prejudice against the pretensions and ostentation of the ruling
class. Their moral viewpoints thus also imply a view of society. In
each case they are contrasted with another character who takes
this flaw to an extreme. On the far side of Darcy is Lady Catherine
de Bourgh, who simply *is* social pride, a woman whose entire
demeanor is designed to keep others in their inferior place.

Elizabeth is an irreverent critic of social superiors, and in this
her model is Mr. Bennet, who has some of the funniest lines and
who spends most of his time amusing himself with the foibles and
nonsense of others. Following his lead, Elizabeth impertinently
defies Lady Catherine. She refuses to accept the comparatively
low position that society has set for her; she uses her wit and
energy to make a place for herself (like Beatrice in *Much Ado About
Nothing*). On the other hand, she is not a Lydia who is openly
defiant and sexually independent.

Both extremes must be avoided. Darcy might end up like Lady
Catherine, whose overbearing manner and self-regard make her
ridiculous; Elizabeth might become her father, who cynically

retreats to the library and refuses to take responsibility for anything. Darcy is aristocracy and Elizabeth is the energy of democracy, but neither appears capable of existing without the counterweight of the other. Elizabeth must outgrow her father. She must move beyond criticism of the pomp of aristocracy to see some of its genuine merits. Darcy must come to appreciate the bumptious energy of the Bennets, while Elizabeth must learn that established authority is not ridiculous simply because it is established.

Review Questions

1. What is Mary Bennet's approach to morals? What is wrong with this?

2. How is Mr. Collins an example of a moral "counterfeit"? How is Wickham a counterfeit?

3. Explain how Austen uses "foils" to develop her moral themes.

4. Discuss some of the complexities of "pride" and "prejudice" in the novel.

5. How is self-knowledge essential to a moral life?

6. How do Darcy and Elizabeth represent different political and social perspectives?

Thought Questions

1. Which daughters does Mrs. Bennet favor? Mr. Bennet? What does this tell us about them?

2. Where do you put Miss Bingley and Mrs. Hurst, Bingley's sisters, on the moral scale?

3. Examine Mr. Collins' proposal to Elizabeth. How does this highlight his role as a moral counterfeit? What kind of proposal does Darcy initially make?

Manners

Manners has two related but distinct senses in Austen. Manners may, on the one hand, refer to the externals of social behavior. Good manners mean conformity to a code of conduct—using the right fork, addressing superiors in the proper manner, holding a door for a lady, sitting up at the table. On the other hand, manners may refer to the way that one treats others in social settings. This is often spoken of as "manner." One's manner (way with other people) is manifested in manners (observance of the code). If one honestly respects and wishes to treat others with dignity, he will observe the small rituals that society imposes. While related, the two can be distinct: It is possible to observe all the rituals and still not possess a kind and warm manner.

In the first respect, Darcy's behavior is unexceptionable. His manners are perfectly polite; his one act of rudeness, his initial comment about Elizabeth, is not intended for her ears. Because of his polished manners, wealth, and good looks, Darcy first makes a favorable impression on everyone. But when they observe his "manners" they change their opinion. This does not mean that he ate with his elbows on the table or that he belched after dinner. Rather what offends is his general demeanor (his *manner*). His approach to people is proud and condescending. As Austen says, his manners "though well-bred, were not inviting." His treatment of Elizabeth is "grave propriety" and politeness (p. 17). Darcy and Bingley are contrasted on this point. Bingley's sisters do not have manners that are equal to his, Elizabeth notes, for Bingley's manners manifest a genuine warmth and invite others into friendship. Bingley, though he is as perfectly well-mannered as Darcy, has something more than politeness: "good humor and kindness" (p. 22).

Manners are a code of communication as well as of behavior. Easy and open manners are signals of a willingness to enter into conversation or dialogue; proud manners are a warning sign that others should keep their distance. The manners with which we treat one another communicate attitudes of generosity or hostility, and function something like a language. Hence Darcy wants to make sure that he does not give any "sign" of admiration, lest he awaken desire in Elizabeth. He makes sure that his "manner" does not communicate affection and that he does not encourage Elizabeth to fall in love with him by his attentions to her.

Manners communicate and shape relations of different classes of society. Tony Tanner points out how important this dimension of manners was in Austen's day, with the threat of French Jacobinism on the horizon:

> It was not a matter of decorum for its own sake: good manners and morals were seen as essential to the preservation of order in society. They alone could or should do what excessive laws, an often recalcitrant militia, and the absence of any properly organized police force were (it was felt) unable to do. It was as if the security and stability of the nation depended on good manners . . . . they were England's answer to the French Revolution.

Manners shape and reinforce the shape of society by marking off one class from another. Rules of manners define the proper approach to a person of higher standing, and thus provide a protective barrier around members of the higher class, which cordons them off from the rest of the world. Darcy is deeply offended when Collins approaches him without introduction, since that is an open transgression of a social boundary. Similarly, Lady Catherine demands that everyone treat her with deferential manners because she is in a higher social position. Miss Bingley and Mrs. Hurst use their manners to display their consciousness of social superiority. Manners communicate the upper class's *différance* from everyone else.

Elizabeth provides a wonderful illustration of both the constraints that the code of manners imposes and also the way a witty and energetic person could use the code to her own advantage. She pokes fun at Darcy's reserve and pride, and shows no proper deference to Lady Catherine. As one critic has said, she "gets away with murder," but she does so without completely abandoning the imposed demands of the code. Though she mocks Darcy, she does not infringe any rules of decorum; she never speaks to him out of turn and does not display the same indifference to propriety that characterizes her mother and sisters. She remains properly respectful toward Lady Catherine, even as she is making her look foolish. She gets angry and indignant, but never throws a fit or loses control of herself. Within the limits imposed by the code of manners, she is capable of expressing a full range of emotions. This variety is in fact one of her virtues; a character, like Wickham, whose manners are the same toward everyone, is using manners to cover up something. After her initial attraction, she eventually finds that Wickham's manners "disgust and weary" her.

Because manners are a code of communication as well as a code of conduct they require interpretation, and this makes the story of *Pride and Prejudice* largely a "hermeneutical drama." Tony Tanner illustrates the necessity for interpretation of manners:

> Consider a ball or a formal dinner. If you subtract the basic purpose of such occasions—to enjoy the pleasures of dancing and eating—you are left with a large superstructure of the occasion which is in effect simply concerned with manners. Apart from the minimal utilitarian purposes (or excuses) for such occasions . . . they are primarily occasions at which manners are demonstrated and celebrated—and tested. They are performances of communal decorum in which society mimes its codes and signs of behavioral values. In themselves they are morally and politically neutral, as the simple act of eating is. Their real importance lies in their being meta-events. Society forgathers to see how society forgathers . . . Their key problem—and drama—arises from the fact that a skillful or well-educated person can, if he or she wishes, deploy and manipulate the signs in such a way that it can become very difficult, if not impossible, to distinguish "true" good manners from adroitly "simulated" ones.

Manners may be misunderstood for a variety of reasons. A scoundrel like Wickham can make his way in good society on the strength of "smooth" manners and charm. Moral insight—an ability to penetrate past the "signs" to the "reality"—is essential. It is also possible to miss obvious clues of behavior or deliberately to ignore the signals and signs that are being communicated. As noted above, Darcy and Elizabeth disagree constantly, and this is not only because of their differing moral stance but because of their different interpretations of manners. In particular, they misinterpret one another's manners. "Mr. Darcy is all politeness," says Elizabeth when he asks her to dance. She thinks he is just showing common courtesy when he is really in love. The drama and irony of the scene depend on our knowing what Elizabeth does not. Here the moral issue of "prejudice" intersects with the interpretation of manners; Elizabeth interprets Darcy's manners wrongly because she has a settled prejudice against him. Likewise, Darcy fails to "exegete" Jane's manner with Bingley correctly. He misconstrues her natural reserve of manner as a sign of her lack of serious interest in Bingley.

Manners are in one sense always a direct manifestation of character. Wickham has a pleasing surface, but when Elizabeth recalls his behavior after reading Darcy's letter, she begins to realize that there were signs of impropriety even in their initial conversations. The clues were there; she simply missed them. On the other hand, Darcy's manners are proud, but there is also a positive dimension to this. It is not that Darcy's manners *hide* his character; it is rather that Elizabeth fails to discern the true nature of his manner and character.

It is important that the transformations of both Darcy and Elizabeth take place, to some degree, "offstage," outside the social setting of balls and conversations. When Elizabeth receives Darcy's letter, she goes away to be alone and enters into a long and revealing self-examination and interior dialogue. Although we do not witness it, Darcy, we may be sure, had gone through something similar after his first proposal. That is the crucial event for both characters. Reflection of this kind is necessary for correct interpretation of the clues that manners afford. We cannot imagine Lydia or Wickham in a reflective moment. Spontaneous and instant interpretation can only lead to error and prejudice. First impressions must be continually checked and revised, and this requires solitude and time.

Though Austen generally upholds the rules of manners, she recognizes a distinction between morally based rules of propriety and rules that are no more than good advice in the majority of cases. Manners have a moral dimension, but not all rules of manner are moral laws. In Austen's day, for example, books of manners for young women discouraged long walks in the open air. (What they would say about women jogging through the neighborhood in spandex can only be imagined.) Elizabeth openly violates this rule in order to visit Jane while she is sick at Netherfield, causing dismay to several other characters. But Elizabeth is right; the good of comforting her sister is far more important than keeping rules about outdoor walks. Elizabeth does not always keep this distinction between rules of manners and moral principles straight.

When Wickham leaves her for Miss King, Elizabeth is so enamored of him that she defends him and classes his action as a breach of propriety. But it is far more: Wickham's behavior proves that he is an unstable character. By refusing to judge him morally, Elizabeth ends up endorsing his conduct and is unprepared for his even more openly immoral conduct with Lydia.

Though there is a distinction between morals and manners there is also a connection, and Elizabeth comes to see this connection in its full weight. Seeing her family through Darcy's eyes, she is embarrassed but she does not see the danger of it. She takes it as merely a breach of etiquette. But then Jane's happiness is ruined because of her family's improprieties and Lydia's continual breaches of small rules of decorum end with a nearly catastrophic moral failing. Elizabeth realizes that protecting the moral tone of the family required protecting the decorum and propriety of their day to day behavior. She rebukes her father for not checking "Lydia's unguarded and imprudent manner." There is also a larger concern underlying this: Without some institutional instruction and control of manners, without the church as a maker of manners, the moral life of the nation will fail.

The moral transformation that takes place in the book is also a transformation of manner. Elizabeth comes to see how easily manners can be misread and how inappropriate manners can lead to real disaster. She concedes that her behavior toward Darcy "was at least always bordering on the uncivil." Darcy for his part sees how proud and disdainful his manner had been, and when Elizabeth visits Pemberly with her relatives, he is quite changed: "more than civil, it was really attentive; and there was no necessity for such attention." As Tave points out, both move toward the perspective of the novel: "principled respect for the rules of decorum, combined with an intelligent realization that merely to obey the rules in their strictest sense does not constitute the whole of good breeding."

Review Questions

1. What are the two senses of *manners*?
2. How are manners like a language?
3. How do manners reinforce the social order of England?
4. Explain *Pride and Prejudice* as a "hermeneutical drama." Why do Darcy and Elizabeth misinterpret one another's manners?
5. Discuss the relationship between moral principles and rules of manners.
6. What is the connection between manners and character?

Thought Questions

1. Before Collins proposes to Elizabeth, she already begins to suspect that he might. How does she draw that conclusion? What does this say about Elizabeth's ability to read people and manners?
2. Discuss the Gardiners in the light of the issues of manners and social position that were examined above. What kind of manners do they have?
3. Why does Elizabeth become angry during Darcy's first proposal? What does it have to do with manners?
4. Examine some passages where Mrs. Bennet is a prominent character. What kind of manners does she display?
5. What are Colonel Fitzwilliam's manners like?
6. How are Darcy's manners different when he meets Elizabeth and the Gardiners at Pemberly? Why?

Marriage and Money

The first sentence of *Pride and Prejudice* is among the most famous lines in English literature. It combines the last of the four *M*s, marriage and money: "It is a truth universally acknowledged, that a single man in possession of a good fortune, must be in want of a wife" (p. 1). Marriage is a key factor in all of Austen's novels, and almost invariably is intertwined with issues of wealth and poverty. This combination has been the source of much misinterpretation of Austen. On the one hand, many read her as a sentimental romantic whose stories always end in predictable marital bliss, while on the other hand some read her as a proto-Marxist who subordinates romance to the practicalities of property and inheritance. It is true that financial considerations have a large place in discussions about marriage, and men are often defined by their income. Austen's vocabulary is frequently taken from finance and trade, even when she is talking about romance. Still, neither of these perspectives is fair to Austen, whose vision of love and marriage is a richly nuanced synthesis of the romantic and the practical.

That marriage is a central concern of *Pride and Prejudice* in particular is evident on the surface of the novel, and the fact that the Bennets stand to lose their home intensifies the girls' need to marry well. A detailed consideration of the literary architecture of the novel reinforces the prominence of these themes. Conversations of Mr. and Mrs. Bennet frame book one, and both are conversations about the Bennet daughters' prospects for marriage. The first chapter is well-known, but the conversation that closes book one is equally funny. Mrs. Bennet is lamenting the fact that Charlotte Lucas has married, and that, by her marriage to Collins, she stands to inherit the Bennet home at Longbourn:

> "Indeed, Mr. Bennet," said she, "it is very hard to think that Charlotte Lucas should ever be mistress of this house, that *I* should be forced to make way for *her*, and live to see her take my place in it!"
>
> "My dear, do not give way to such gloomy thoughts. Let us

hope for better things. Let us flatter ourselves that *I* may be the survivor."

This was not very consoling to Mrs. Bennet, and, therefore, instead of making any answer, she went on as before.

"I cannot bear to think that they should have all this estate. If it was not for the entail I should not mind it."

"What should you not mind?"

"I should not mind anything at all."

"Let us be thankful that you are preserved from a state of such insensibility." (pp. 91–92)

Between these two dialogues in book one, romances are initiated, two potential romances are broken off, and another is left hanging:

> Mr. and Mrs. Bennet
> > Bingley and Darcy arrive in Netherfield: Hopes for Jane
> > > Collins: Hopes for Elizabeth
> > > > Wickham
> > > Collins proposes: dashes hopes for Elizabeth
> > Bingley and Darcy leave: dashes hopes for Jane
> Mr. and Mrs. Bennet

Book one thus arranges various characters in matching pairs. Darcy and Bingley are first introduced and Mrs. Bennet has high hopes that Jane and Bingley will marry. Collins appears and there are hopes for Elizabeth and Collins. After Wickham's appearance at the center of the book, the two romances unravel in reverse order. Elizabeth rejects Collins' proposal, and then Bingley and Darcy quit Netherfield, dashing hopes for Jane. The first book leaves the relationship of Wickham and Elizabeth unrealized, and this romance is rolled into book two.

If book one treated Jane and Elizabeth equally, book two focuses more clearly on the latter. We follow her movements as she goes from Longbourn to Rosings for a visit with Charlotte Lucas, and back to Longbourn. During book two, it becomes evident that Wickham is not going to pursue Elizabeth, which brings an end to the unresolved romance of book one. With Darcy's proposal to Elizabeth at the center of book two, another romance is initiated, to be left unresolved into book three.

Longbourn
    Jane and Bingley
        Jane leaves
    Elizabeth and Wickham
        Elizabeth leaves
Rosings
    Lady Catherine
        Darcy's proposal - center of book two
    Darcy's letter; Elizabeth's reevaluation of Wickham
Longbourn
    Lydia takes center stage on trip home
        Lydia leaves
    Elizabeth leaves with Gardiners

Book three is full of resolutions. The three main women characters are engaged or married in ascending order of importance, and with increasing property: Lydia to Wickham, Jane to Bingley, and finally Elizabeth to Darcy. Spatial movements are again structurally important: Elizabeth's visit to Pemberly at the beginning anticipates her permanent residence at Pemberly at the end of the book, and is in fact the means for realizing that permanent residence.

Pemberly
    Elizabeth and Gardiners
    Darcy's appearance
    Jane's letter
Longbourn
    Lydia's crisis
        Lydia and Wickham to Longbourn
            Gardiner's letter: Darcy's role in Wickham affair revealed
        Lydia and Wickham leave
Bingley, Darcy again at Netherfield, concluding what began in bk. one
    Jane's marriage arranged
    Elizabeth's marriage arranged

Throughout her writing career, Austen was critical of romantic notions of love. *Northanger Abbey*, as I discuss in the next chapter, is a parody of the romance genre that was so popular in Austen's day. She exposes the evils of extreme sensibility and sentimentality in *Sense and Sensibility*. These themes are important also to *Pride and Prejudice*. The original title of the novel was "First Impressions," which hints that the book is a treatment of the romantic convention of "love at first sight." Austen, however, inverts the standard romantic story. Elizabeth's first impressions of Darcy and Wickham are both mistaken. This is not love at first sight; rather, it presents the thesis that love often comes only after a second or third look. You cannot trust first impressions, or the surface of manners. Time and intelligence are needed to see what kind of "manner" is being expressed by the manners, and then penetrate further to the "character" of the person. Austen has very specific ideas about love, romance, and marriage, but as in other cases, she is not simplistic. She gives a complex taxonomy of different approaches to marriage and love. She is not a Mrs. Bennet, who thinks *every* marriage, no matter how imprudent, is good. Instead of giving us a simple twelve-step guide to a happy marriage, Austen presents a complex spectrum of marital possibilities.

The first marriage presented to us is the elder Bennets. The opening and closing dialogues of book one display the characteristic tone of the marriage. Mrs. Bennet is flighty, nervous, violently overanxious, while Mr. Bennet is alternately exasperated and amused by her behavior. He escapes from her as much as possible, spending time in his library with his books, which have the virtue of not being loud; and when he is with her, he mocks her and enjoys the mockery all the more because she is completely unaware of it.

How did they get into such a state? We get some hints of the origins of their marriage later in the book. Mrs. Bennet is lamenting the departure of the soldiers from Meryton and "she remembered what she had herself endured on a similar occasion, five and twenty years ago," when she cried for two days after a regiment left her area (p. 157). This was only a couple of years before she married Mr. Bennet, and this is the kind of background she brought into the marriage. She was, in short, a hopeless flirt, a Lydia. On Mr. Bennet's side, he was "captivated by youth and beauty, and that appearance of good humour, which youth and beauty generally give" (p. 162). Attracted by her liveliness, Mr. Bennet failed to consider his wife-to-be's "weak understanding and illiberal mind." Their marriage was a marriage of passion, but a marriage that did not involve a meeting of minds.

The result of such a marriage is little short of disaster. There is no picture of "conjugal felicity or domestic comfort" in the Bennet home (p. 162) and Elizabeth is reluctantly forced to admit to Lady Catherine that her sisters have not been required to study. Mr. Bennet's retreat from the marriage involves a retreat from responsibilities to his daughters, and Elizabeth rightly discerns that Wickham was emboldened to run away with Lydia because he observed her father's indolence and indifference. Mr. Bennet does not take the steps necessary to protect his family from financial ruin, always hoping for the son who never came. The sins of the father are carried out in the next generation. Mr. Bennet escapes without falling into ruin, but only by Darcy's intervention. The near-disasters of the Bennet family began with the father's decision to marry an inappropriate partner.

Wickham's marriage to Lydia is of a similar kind. She is a younger version of her mother, full of violent joy and laughter. Her letter to Mrs. Foster displays her complete lack of concern for propriety, foresight, planning, or practical considerations:

> You will laugh when you know where I am gone, and I cannot help laughing myself at your surprise tomorrow morning, as soon as I am missed. I am going to Gretna Green, and if you cannot guess with who, I shall think you a simpleton, for there is but one man in the world I love, and he is an angel. I should never be happy without him, so think it no harm to be off. You need not send them word at Longbourn of my going, if you do not like it, for it will make the surprise greater, when I write to them, and sign my name Lydia Wickham. What a good joke it will be! I can hardly write for laughing. (p. 199)

Lydia reduces her marriage, even a scandalous marriage causing grief to her whole family, to a joke. She, not Elizabeth, is the
kind of person who makes everything look ridiculous because she
thinks life is a joke. As for Wickham, Mrs. Gardiner comments
that at least he did not pick out Lydia for money, but his total lack
of concern for the practicalities, the morality, and the propriety of
his relationship with Lydia is an evil. Elizabeth is right to wonder
"how Wickham and Lydia were to be supported in tolerable independence" and she thinks of "how little of permanent happiness
could belong to a couple who were only brought together because
their passions were stronger than their virtue" (p. 214). We can
easily imagine the Wickhams twenty years hence, because we have
already seen the Bennets.

These are "imprudent" marriages, the product of nothing more
than overpowering passion and characterized by folly and lack of
foresight. The evident flaws in these marriages may suggest that
Austen wants us to favor the practical marriage, the managed
marriage, the calculated marriage, the marriage whose purpose is
to advance economic or social status. Interestingly, these two vi-
sions of marriage are not wholly distinct; Mrs. Bennet especially
hopes for marriage for her daughters partly because she wants
them to have a "good fortune," but she is foolishly satisfied with
any marriage at all.

Critical as Austen is of imprudent marriage, she is sufficiently
romantic to detest the advantageous marriage with equal intensity. We see several attempts at "prudent" marriages in the novel,
and one prudent marriage actually concluded. None of it is pretty.
Both Bingley and Darcy are being manipulated into marriages
that will bring social and economic advantage. Jane quotes a letter from Caroline Bingley that says her brother is intended for
Miss Darcy and that the whole family desires it. Caroline wants
Bingley to marry Darcy's sister because it would promote her plan
to grab Mr. Darcy. Wickham informs Elizabeth early on that Darcy
is intended for Miss de Bourgh, a marriage that would unite the
two estates and two great families. Lady Catherine treats the relationship as a virtual engagement.

The one prudent marriage we actually see is that of Charlotte Lucas and Mr. Collins. Before Mr. Collins has appeared, Charlotte informs Elizabeth that she intends to enter marriage for advantage, without regard to love. Charlotte believes it is better for husband and wife not to know one another very well before marriage; since they will grow unlike afterward, any knowledge of disposition before the marriage is irrelevant. When she actually chooses to marry, it is on precisely these principles. After Elizabeth refuses Mr. Collins' proposal, Charlotte contrives to stay in the room while Mr. Collins is talking with Mrs. Bennet, and later when she "perceived [Collins] from an upper window as he walked towards the house" she "instantly set out to meet him accidentally in the lane" (p. 85). Charlotte is "not romantic" and only wants a "comfortable home." The protective shield provided by the institution of marriage is more important than the particular man she happens to be married to. Though she starts at the opposite end of the spectrum from Mrs. Bennet, she ends up with the same conclusion: marriage is good is good is good.

Passion is an insecure foundation for marriage, but calculating prudence is equally so. Though beginning from the opposite pole from the Bennets, Charlotte's marriage to Collins ends up very like the Bennets. Collins likes to work in the garden and Charlotte encourages him, supposedly because he needs the exercise. Her real intention, of course, is to keep him as far away as possible for as long as possible. Charlotte, moreover, makes her "headquarters" in a back room that is not really suitable, merely to get away from him. She is retreating from her husband as soon as the marriage begins because, like Mr. Bennet, she finds her partner embarrassing. Collins is too much the blockhead to recognize what is going on, and he boasts of the deep intimacy and communion of taste that he shares with Charlotte. Clearly, Austen is not recommending such a conclusion, but she is gentle with Charlotte. Charlotte is "forced" to this position: in Austen's world, there is not much alternative for a plain young woman of modest inheritance.

Austen presents failed marriages that arise out of folly and passion, and failed marriages that are arranged for purely financial or
social gain. But she also gives us several good matches, and these
all share certain characteristics. First, a sound marriage does not
ignore practical matters of finances and social position. Darcy is
not wrong to consider the prudence of a marriage to Elizabeth, or
to be concerned with the behavior of Elizabeth's family. He can
see where the improprieties of Lydia are leading and rightly wants
to preserve his family name from associations with scandal. Nor is
it wrong for Elizabeth to consider the comfort of her life with Mr.
Darcy. Seeing Pemberly is an important stage in the development
of her affection for Darcy, and in part she is attracted because to
be mistress of Pemberly would be something. Second, the good
matches are based on physical attraction. Darcy is attracted to
Elizabeth not only for her liveliness and wit, but also for her "fine
eyes," and everyone in the book agrees that Darcy is a remarkably
good-looking man. Sexual attraction is not very openly expressed
in Austen's novels, whether due to social constraints or to personal reticence, but Austen knows that sexual attraction is an in-
dispensable feature of romantic love.

Beyond this, however, a good match is founded on a bond of
taste and feeling. One of the main problems with both the romantic marriage of the Bennets and the prudent marriage of the
Collinses is that they breed a lack of respect. When Elizabeth examines her feelings for Darcy late in the novel, she discovers that
they are a combination of gratitude, respect, and honor. Especially after Darcy's intervention to assist Lydia and Wickham, Elizabeth declares that she is "proud" of him. Such feelings are not
based on first impressions, nor is simply based on calculations of
economic advantage. There is calculation involved, but it is calculation of character rather than wealth; a good match rests on recognizing the *moral* advantage that each person would bring to the
other.

During her visit to Pemberly, moreover, Elizabeth begins to
recognize how much she shares of Darcy's taste. She is not impressed so much by its size and richness as by the taste and beauty.
Touring the house, she looks out a window at the grounds:

The hill, crowned with wood, from which they had descended, receiving increased abruptness from the distance, was a beautiful object. Every disposition of the ground was good; and she looked on the whole scene, the river, the trees scattered on its banks, and the winding of the valley, as far as she could trace it, with delight. As they passed into other rooms, these objects were taking different positions; but from every window there were beauties to be seen. The rooms were lofty and handsome, and their furniture suitable to the fortune of their proprietor; but Elizabeth saw, with admiration of his taste, that it was neither gaudy nor uselessly fine; with less of splendor, and more real elegance, than the furniture of Rosings. (p. 167)

Darcy's house is an extension of his character, and Elizabeth's delight in Pemberly is part of her growing interest in and admiration for the owner.

Communion of taste does not mean that a husband and wife become interchangeable. Darcy and Elizabeth will always be different, but their differences will harmonize rather than conflict. Elizabeth sees that their differences will bring advantage to both: "by her ease and liveliness, his mind might have been softened, his manners improved, and from his judgment, information, and knowledge of the world, she must have received benefit of even greater importance" (p. 214). To Darcy's high purpose and gravity, Elizabeth brings laughter.

Early in the book, Charlotte Lucas states her opinion that "Happiness in marriage is entirely a matter of chance" (p. 15). As it happens, this is ironic, for she definitely does not leave anything to chance in securing Mr. Collins. But her opinion seems to be Austen's own. She is realist enough to know that achieving marital happiness has a serendipitous quality. Planning is important, but happiness cannot be controlled or planned for with any certainty. For Elizabeth and Darcy, love comes to her as a surprise, as a gift, as an act of "grace."

Review Questions

1. Is Austen a romantic, a Marxist, neither, or both?

2. Describe how the Bennet marriage began. What is the result of that marriage?

3. How is the marriage of Lydia and Wickham like that of the Bennets?

4. What kind of courtship do Charlotte and Mr. Collins have? What is the result?

5. What are the elements of a good marriage?

Thought Questions

1. We see several good marriages in the making in *Pride and Prejudice*. Are any of the mature marriages good matches? Which ones? What makes them good matches?

2. Compare and contrast the marriage of Jane and Bingley with that of Elizabeth and Darcy. What will the two marriages be like in twenty years?

3. Why does Wickham pursue Miss King for a time? What does this say about his notions of love and marriage?

CHAPTER 3

"What Ideas Have You Been Admitting?":
Northanger Abbey

Northanger Abbey works on several levels at once. On the one hand, it is a straightforward love story about the young Catherine Morland and her romance with Henry Tilney. As is usual in Austen's novels, the romance is endangered in various ways but these all work toward a comic conclusion. *Northanger Abbey* is also a novel of education. At the beginning, Catherine is ignorant in nearly every way. She has spent her first seventeen years at home and her small experience of the world has not been increased by reading, since she avoids "books of information" and reads only books that contain "nothing like useful knowledge," which are "all story and no reflection" (p. 9).[†] Through her experience in Bath, and under Henry's instruction, she becomes more discerning. The education he gives her consists largely of learning the truth about the illusions that have distorted her view of the world. Significantly, Henry is a pastor who, unlike Collins in *Pride and Prejudice*, actually provides guidance toward virtue.

The book consists of two parts which are united by their concern for different forms of illusion and their correction. In the first half, Catherine learns about the deceptions and lies that are part of social life and begins to judge people accurately. In the second half, Catherine is forced to confront her own delusions, which have been shaped by her reading of romance literature and especially Gothic romance.

[†] Page numbers are from the Konemann edition (1999).

Overlapping these dimensions of the novel—the straightforward love story and the novel of education—is a parody of Gothic romance. *Parody* and *Gothic romance* are terms that perhaps require more explanation. First, a parody is a work of literature that imitates another work or author in order to make fun of it. Parody is sometimes sharply critical of the work that it is imitating, but often the mockery is in good humor and is not an attack on the original work. Henry Beard's delightful *Poetry for Cats: The Definitive Anthology of Distinguished Feline Verse* provides some wonderful examples. Beard writes parodies of several dozen major poems from English and American literature, rewriting the original poems as if they had been written by the poet's cat. Here is the original first stanza of William Blake's "The Tyger":

> Tyger, Tyger, burning bright,
> In the forests of the night;
> What immortal hand or eye,
> Could frame thy fearful symmetry?

Here is Beard's parody, written by "William Blake's Cat":

> Mongrel! Mongrel! Barking blight,
> Bane upon my yard at night;
> What infernal hand or eye,
> Could frame thy vile anatomy?

Beard follows Blake's rhymes and meter but inverts the point of the poem. Instead of a mysterious meditation on the "Tyger," the poem becomes a comic attack on dogs.

In particular, Austen is poking fun at the Gothic romance, a particular kind of novel that was popular in her time. Henry Tilney provides a good example of the atmosphere and events typical of Gothic romance. As Henry drives Catherine toward Northanger Abbey, his family's home, he scares Catherine with stories of the horrors that await her at the Abbey:

> "On the second, or at farthest the *third* night after your arrival, you will probably have a violent storm. Peals of thunder so

loud as to seem to shake the edifice to its foundations will roll round the neighbouring mountains . . . .Unable of course to repress your curiosity in so favourable a moment for indulging it, you will instantly arise, and, throwing your dressing-gown around you, proceed to examine this mystery. After a very short search, you will discover a division in the tapestry so artfully constructed as to defy the minutest inspection, and on opening it, a door will immediately appear, which door being only secured by massy bars and a padlock, you will, after a few efforts, succeed in opening, and, with your lamp in your hand, will pass through it into a small vaulted room. . . .

"You will proceed into this small vaulted room, and through this into several others, without perceiving anything very remarkable in either. In one, perhaps, there may be a dagger, in another a few drops of blood, and in a third the remains of some instrument of torture . . . your eyes will be attracted towards a large, old-fashioned cabinet of ebony and gold, which, though narrowly examining the furniture before, you had passed unnoticed . . . . At last . . . by touching a secret spring, an inner compartment will open, a roll of paper appears, you seize it,—it contains many sheets of manuscript,—you hasten with the precious treasure into your own chamber; but scarcely have you been able to decipher, 'Oh thou, whomsoever thou mayest be, into whose hands these memoirs of the wretched Matilda may fall,'—when your lamp suddenly expires in the socket and leaves you in total darkness." (pp. 143–144)

If you have seen horror movies from the 1950s, you know the type of story.

The effectiveness of parody lies partly in the expectations of readers. For someone who knows Blake's poem, the first line of Beard's parody is both familiar and comically unfamiliar, and the parody is funny largely because of the interplay between familiarity and unfamiliarity. Cervantes' *Don Quixote* similarly draws much of its humor from the readers' expectation that a knight should be youthful, strong, and useful—none of which describes the Don. Austen's parody functions the same way. Readers come to the novel with certain expectations about how the story will go, what kinds of characters they will meet, and the eventual outcome. Austen undermines those expectations at every turn, giving us a heroine who does not live up to the role, a hero who is witty and wise but not dashingly handsome, and an old castle that holds no secrets.

One of the intriguing things about Austen's book is that she is constantly "checking" her story against a model, and finding that it does not live up to its genre. She is constantly saying, "I know you readers are expecting thus and so, but what happens in my story is this and such." This has several important effects. First, it makes it possible for a reader who has never heard of Gothic romance to make sense of Austen's parody. Second, it makes it clear that Austen herself knew an awful lot about Gothic romance. We know from her letters that she read and enjoyed the novels of Anne Radcliffe and others, and this is evident in her own novel. This fact helps us understand the point of her parody; if she is *attacking* Gothic, how does she know so much about it?

Austen's effort to write a parody that is also a novel in its own right presented her with a number of difficulties. The book is a novel and an anti-novel, a romance and a parody of romance pressed into two covers. As a result, some critics claim, the novel has no real drama since we are never allowed to get close to the characters. We are always viewing them as *characters* in a Gothic romance, because from the opening lines to the closing, the narrator keeps reminding us that they are characters in a Gothic romance. Characters fill the roles that are necessary for a romantic fiction but never come alive as individuals. We are always at a distance, smiling condescendingly at their folly; we never *feel* their folly as we do Elizabeth Bennet's in *Pride and Prejudice*.

Added to this is the problem of Austen's youth as a writer. Though *Northanger Abbey* was not published until after Austen's death, it was one of the first novels she wrote and is similar in many respects to parodies she wrote as a teenager. Her immaturity is evident in several ways. Roger Gard has pointed out that Austen often makes the comedy too obvious. He cites an example from the first part of the book, where Mrs. Allen, a neighbor of the Morlands who is supervising Catherine during her trip to

Bath, meets an old friend at the Pump House, a public gathering place in the city: "The joy of this meeting was very great, as well it might, since they had been content to know nothing of each other for the last fifteen years" (p. 23). Austen's description is amusing, but Gard argues that "This is not rich irony, but sarcasm. And, as is often the case with sarcasm, no one needs it. The tone, interestingly, is near to that of the young person who just cannot believe how *incredibly* stupid (and so forth) middle-aged people can be."

Catherine especially is criticized as an inconsistent or unbelievable character. William Dean Howells said that she is a "goose," but hastily added, as if to soften his criticism, that she is "a very engaging goose." Apparent inconsistency in her character is more of a problem. On the one hand, she is introduced as being wholly unimaginative: "She could never learn or understand anything before she was taught; and sometimes not even then, for she was often inattentive and occasionally stupid" (pp. 7–8). By the middle of the novel, however, she has become so full of imaginative flights that she has to be rebuked for being too fanciful.

These criticisms have some weight, but some of them are simply misguided, and the novel is still successful in spite of it all. The idea that Catherine is inconsistent, for example, fails to recognize the progression of Catherine's experience. She does indeed start out dull and unimaginative, but at Bath she comes under the influence of Isabella Thorpe, who introduces her to romantic fiction, fills her head full of Gothic horrors and expectations, and who "sounds like all the heroines of [Catherine's] acquaintance." In short, Catherine grows *into* a fanciful young woman before she grows *out* of that stage. Further, both aspects of the novel— Catherine's introduction to Bath social life and Catherine's renunciation of Gothic fantasies—are aspects of a single set of issues, the issues of accurate sight and correct interpretation, which are recurring themes in all of Austen's work.

So, this double plot movement is crucial for the moral education that Catherine undergoes and the moral education Austen hoped to lead her readers through. She begins the novel naive and susceptible to influence. As she begins to read Gothic romances, she is filled with fears about strange and unutterable horrors. But in becoming attentive to bizarre horrors, she overlooks the real villainy that is right before her, the much more common villainy of John and Isabella Thorpe. Austen knows that the evils that Catherine actually faces are much more like the evils that her readers face. Few readers of *Northanger Abbey* have an insane ex-wife locked in the attic or mother's skeleton buried in the basement; few even know someone who has. Most readers of the novel, however, will have met more than their share of Johns and Isabellas and General Tilneys. Learning to deal with the latter is the real context for ethical progress. As Tave points out, "to live the common life well is uncommon." Pressing the romance and the anti-romance into a single set of covers is essential if Austen is going to make this point well.

Structurally, the two parts of the novel parallel one another. Austen begins, as we shall see, with overt references to the romance genre, self-consciously pointing out that her heroine and her book will violate all the rules of Gothic fiction. As part one progresses, however, we almost forget the parody as Catherine becomes involved with the Thorpes and the Tilneys. Early in part two Catherine changes location, as the story moves to Northanger Abbey, the ancestral home of the Tilneys, where Catherine has been invited as a guest. There her Gothic fantasies come to a climax until she is sharply rebuked and mortified by Henry Tilney. From that point the story again moves in a more "realistic" direction, focusing on the developing romance between Henry and Catherine and the obstacles that remain standing in their way. Part one moves from Gothic to realistic, and part two does the same.

Another structural principle is at work in the novel: The parallels between three sets of siblings. Catherine and her brother James are one pair, and they fall in with John and Isabella Thorpe while they are staying in Bath. The relationships between these sets of siblings dominate the first half of the book, and the issue here has to do with the social delusions that are symbolized and represented by John and Isabella. The other pair is Henry and Eleanor

Tilney, who become more dominant in the second half of the book. The shift from Thorpes to the Tilneys is a mark of Catherine's progress.

This structure might leave the impression that Austen's point is to expose the silliness of Gothic romance. It might appear that Austen has written a novel that is teaching us all to learn to be "realistic" and to outgrow fiction. But this is not Austen's point. Writing a novel to condemn fiction and imagination would be unusual, to say the least, and there are several passages where the narrator and various characters explicitly defend novels, including Gothic novels. For Austen, the relationship between fiction and reality is far more subtle, and imagination has an important place in learning to live well. As we shall see, there are even signs in the novel that Austen believed that fiction, and Gothic romance in particular, made an important contribution to moral development.

Review Questions

1. What are the two levels of *Northanger Abbey*?
2. What is a parody?
3. What are some of the common elements of Gothic romance fiction?
4. What are some of the criticisms of the novel?
5. Does the novel hang together as a unity?
6. What is the structure of the novel?

Part One: Bath

From the first paragraph it is obvious that Austen is playing off of the conventions of Gothic novels:

No one who had ever seen Catherine Morland in her infancy would have supposed her born to be a heroine. Her situation in life, the character of her father and mother, her own person and disposition, were all equally against her. Her father was a clergyman, without being neglected, or poor, and a very respectable man, though he name was Richard—and he had never been handsome. He had a considerable independence, besides two good livings—and he was not in the least addicted to locking up his daughters. Her mother was a woman of useful, plain sense, with a good temper, and, what is more remarkable, with a good constitution. She had three sons before Catherine was born; and, instead of dying in bringing the latter into the world, as anybody might expect, she still lived on—lived to have six children more— to see them growing up around her, and to enjoy excellent health herself. (p. 7)

Catherine's adventures are likewise the antithesis of romance adventures. Austen's record of her parting from her family to Bath is layered with the same irony:

It is remarkable . . . that [Mrs. Morland] never insisted on Catherine's writing by every post, nor exacted her promise of transmitting the character of every new acquaintance, nor a detail of every interesting conversation that Bath might produce. Everything indeed relative to this important journey was done on the part of the Morlands with a degree of moderation and composure, which seemed rather consistent with the common feelings of common life, than with the refined susceptibilities, the tender emotions which the first separation of a heroine from her family ought always to excite. Her father, instead of giving her an unlimited order on his banker, or even putting a hundred pounds bank-bill into her hands, gave her only ten guineas, and promised her more when she wanted it.

Under these unpromising auspices, the parting took place, and the journey began. It was performed with suitable quietness and uneventful safety. Neither robbers nor tempests befriended them, nor one lucky overturn to introduce them to the hero. Nothing more alarming occurred than a fear, on Mrs. Allen's side, of having once left her clogs behind her at an inn, and that fortunately proved to be groundless. (pp. 12–13)

Austen's parody of stock conventions of romance are often more subtle. Rachel Brownstein summarizes a few:

Catherine's necessary hero is introduced to her altogether prosaically, as a dancing partner, by the master of ceremonies whose job it is to make such introductions. Romantic fiction is implicitly debunked by this even, also by the fact that Catherine likes Henry Tilney immediately, and that makes him like her: far from being overwhelmed by her heroinical qualities, "a persuasion of her partiality for him [is] the only cause of giving her a serious thought." The tropes of stock romance are parodied as, for instance, the requisite separation of the lovers is effected by Isabella Thorpe and her brother John, who physically restrain Catherine, each holding onto one arm, when she struggles to follow Henry and his sister down the street. Longing for the more elegant Tilneys, our heroine is entangled with the vulgar Thorpes, because she was so quickly taken up by the importunate, scheming Isabella.

The parody here is obvious, but what is less obvious is the fact that Austen is not only being ironic about Gothic romance, but is being ironic about her own parody of romance. In the opening paragraph, Austen addresses readers who expect all heroines to be beautiful, to have dashingly handsome but cruel fathers, to suffer under some extreme injustice or obstacle to happiness, to have fathers with names other than "Richard." Only such readers are among the "anybody" who expect the mother of the heroine to die in childbirth. But the irony is at least three layers thick. Austen is not really addressing readers who have such expectations; she is *pretending* to address those kinds of readers, and by making the assumptions so explicit she is showing that she expects readers will *not* have those expectations. Or, better—and this is yet another layer of irony—she is addressing readers who think that *other* readers have these expectations. She is inviting readers to join with her little joke, her joke at the expense of readers of Gothic romance. Finally, in the crowning irony, though Austen says that no one would expect Catherine to be a heroine of a romance, that is in fact what she is. These layers of irony should make us cautious about evaluating Austen's novel. If we think we are reading a straightforward rejection of Gothic romance, we should suspect that we missed something.

Though Austen is mocking certain features of Gothic novels, *Northanger Abbey* is clearly not an anti-novel novel. During her time in Bath, Catherine spends time reading novels with Isabella, and this occasions a passionate (if still ironic) outburst from the narrator, protesting the novelists' self-destructive attack on novels:

> Yes, novels; —for I will not adopt that ungenerous and impolitic custom so common with novel writers, of degrading by their contemptuous censure the very performances, to the number of which they are themselves adding—joining with their greatest enemies in bestowing the harshest epithets on such works, and scarcely ever permitting them to be read by their own heroine, who, if she accidentally take up a novel, is sure to turn over its insipid pages with disgust. . . . there seems to be almost a general wish of decrying the capacity and undervaluing the labour of the novelist, and of slighting those performances which have only genius, wit, and taste to recommend them. (p. 29)

The characters of *Northanger Abbey* may in fact be evaluated by their taste in fiction. John Thorpe, the clear "antihero" of the novel, despises Gothic romance, while the hero, Henry Tilney, a man of good education and refined taste, claims that he read *Udolpho* with his hair standing on end. Not every reader of romances is a good character, but refusing to read romance is a sure mark of a stunted imagination. Austen is exploring the limitations of this kind of fiction, but she is also recognizing its value.

As mentioned above, part one focuses attention on Catherine's education in social life, which begins with her visit to Bath. In Austen's day, Bath was one of the most fashionable resorts in England, and Catherine, whose social life has involved only some forty-odd families in her home village, is agog at the bustling wonders of the city. Given her sheltered upbringing in a minister's family, Catherine was not prepared for the deceptions that are so much a part of high social life in Bath. She needs to have another guide, another shepherd, to guide her through.

Almost immediately, she meets that guide: Henry Tilney.

After they have danced at the Pump Room, he initiates a parody of a first conversation:

> "I have hitherto been very remiss, madam, in the proper attentions of a partner here; I have not yet asked you how long you have been in Bath; whether you were ever here before; whether you have been at the Upper Rooms, the theatre, and the concert; and how you like the place altogether. I have been very negligent—but are you now at leisure to satisfy me in these particulars? If you are, I will begin directly."
>
> "You need not give yourself that trouble, sir."
>
> "No trouble, I assure you, madam." Then, forming his features into a set smile, and affectedly softening his voice, he added, with a simpering air, "Have you been long in Bath, madam?"
>
> "About a week, sir," replied Catherine, trying not to laugh.
>
> "Really!" with affected astonishment.
>
> "Why should you be surprised, sir?"
>
> "Why, indeed!" said he, in his natural tone: "but some emotion must appear to be raised by your reply, and surprise is more easily assumed, and not less reasonable than any other.—Now let us go on. Were you ever here before, madam?"
>
> "Never, sir."
>
> "Indeed! Have you yet honoured the Upper Rooms?"
>
> "Yes, sir; I was there last Monday."
>
> "Have you been to the theatre?"
>
> "Yes, sir; I was at the play on Tuesday."
>
> "To the concert?"
>
> "Yes, sir; on Wednesday."
>
> "And are you altogether pleased with Bath?"
>
> "Yes—I like it very well."
>
> "Now I must give one smirk, and then we may be rational again."
>
> Catherine turned away her head, not knowing whether she might venture to laugh. (pp. 18–19)

This initial conversation sets the tone of the relationship between Catherine and Henry. Throughout the novel, Henry is, like Austen herself, a satirist, poking fun at the conventions of social life. In his ironic way, however, Henry is beginning to teach

Catherine. By leading her through this conversation he both shows her the "way it's done in Bath" and also exposes how shallow and deceptive Bath is. Though playfully said, this is the chief lesson that Catherine will have to learn.

Catherine is attracted to Henry after their first conversation, where his wit and irony leave her as confused as she is amused. It is only after this conversation and her growing interest in Henry that she meets John and Isabella Thorpe, the son and daughter of Mrs. Thorpe, an old though forgotten friend of Mrs. Allen. This sequence—Henry first, then the Thorpes—is important in two respects. First, it means that John Thorpe comes onto the scene where a romance is already taking shape and takes the role of a rival suitor. His attempt to detach Catherine from Henry is not an attempt to prevent a romance from beginning; it is a much more vicious attempt to destroy a romance already begun. Second, this sequence indicates that even before Catherine is faced with the test and challenge of the Thorpes, she has already been introduced to the man who will guide her to success in that test.

The Thorpes pose a challenge to the naive Catherine because both of them remake reality according to their imagination. John is the more obvious of the two, boasting about his horses and his successes in a thoroughly disagreeable but often very funny way. During one outing with Catherine, he entertains her with tales of his prowess:

> He told her of horses which he had bought for a trifle and sold for incredible sums; of racing matches in which his judgment had infallibly foretold the winner; of shooting parties, in which he had killed more birds (though without having one good shot) than all his companions together; and described to her some famous day's sport, with the fox-hounds, in which his foresight and skill in directing the dogs had repaired the mistakes of the most experienced huntsman, and in which the boldness of his riding, though it had never endangered his own life for a moment, had been constantly leading others into difficulties, which he calmly concluded had broken the necks of many. (p. 58)

Hardly what one would call a "dream date." The contrast with Henry is striking; while Henry displays a nearly feminine knowledge of romance novels and the qualities of muslin, John is a parody of the manly sportsman. Even the sheltered Catherine senses that there is something wrong with the man, though she lacks so much confidence in her judgment that she can only consider him "not altogether agreeable."

John Thorpe becomes much more that "not altogether agreeable" when he deliberately manipulates and deceives Catherine more than once. On the first, he insists that Catherine should accompany him to Clarenton Downs, though she is reluctant to go. On another occasion, he lies to her about the Tilneys in order to get her to accompany him to Blaize Castle. He claims that he had seen the Tilneys riding off in another direction, but as soon as he and Catherine are in the coach and heading for the castle, they see the Tilneys walking to keep their appointment with Catherine. On a third occasion, Thorpe again wants Catherine to be with him when she has made plans to spend time with the Tilneys, and this time Thorpe goes so far as to visit the Tilneys to make Catherine's excuses for her. Ultimately, this turns out well for Catherine. She breaks away from the Thorpes and marches to the Tilneys to inform them of John's lie. As a result, she meets General Tilney for the first time and receives her first invitation to dinner. Despite the good outcome, it rapidly becomes clear that John is a liar and a cheat, and Catherine is on her guard afterwards. By seeing through John, Catherine passes the first part of her Bath test.

Just as much as her brother, Isabella shapes the world to her own desires and expectations, manipulating and flirting her way to success. Her manipulations are less overt than her brother's and thus more dangerous. Catherine is uncomfortable around John from the beginning, but has to learn to see through Isabella's false exterior. Clues to Isabella's character are not hard to come by if Catherine had eyes to see. Isabella complains about some young men who are watching her and pretends to want to get away from them, but then contrives to meet them on the street. She tells

Catherine that she plans to sit and talk through a whole evening, but spends most of the evening dancing with Henry Tilney's brother, Captain Tilney. This track record of hypocrisy and duplicity is clear enough to the reader, and there is no surprise when she abandons James Morland for Captain Tilney. It takes Catherine completely by surprise. She cannot imagine that people could say one thing and do another. Faced with these circumstances and people, as Tave points out, Catherine is continually finding Bath "odd" and "alarming." Simpleminded as she is, she is baffled by life and continually surprised when life overtakes her.

Catherine's initial inability to see through the illusions and deceptions of Bath society, and especially the deceptions of the Thorpes, is connected to the question of literature in a couple of ways. John Thorpe dismisses romances, but speaks highly of *The Monk*, a book far more lurid and unrealistic than any of the books that Catherine reads. Isabella claims to be a great reader of romance novels, and she talks like all the heroines that Catherine has read about. In short, Isabella is a romance heroine, and Catherine's learning to see through her is of a piece with her learning to see through the illusions of romance literature.

One of the key conversations of part one takes place in chapter fourteen. It begins as a discussion concerning the proper use of language. Catherine expresses astonishment that Henry is a reader of romances, assuming that "young men despised novels amazingly" (p. 97). Henry corrects her mistake, but also gently teases her about the use of "amazingly." Catherine has said that men "despised . . . amazingly," and Henry responds "It is *amazingly*; it may well suggest *amazement* if they do—for they read nearly as many as women." His instruction in language continues when Catherine calls *Uldopho* "the nicest book in the world." Henry pretends to be uncertain as to what she means by "nicest": "I suppose you mean the neatest. That must depend on the binding." When Eleanor objects to Henry's impertinence, he fills out his critique:

> "Very true," said Henry, "and this is a very nice day; and we are taking a very nice walk; and you are two very nice young ladies.

Oh, it is a very nice word, indeed!—it does for everything. Originally, perhaps, it was applied only to express neatness, propriety, delicacy, or refinement; —people were nice in their dress, in their sentiments, or their choice. But now every commendation on every subject is comprised in that one word." (p. 98)

Several things are going on in this scene. First, Austen is using "props" to highlight and fill out character. Books and reading habits are the subject of discussion, and the various characters show their colors by describing the kind of books they most enjoy. Catherine reads little besides romance and considers history to be merely for the torment of schoolchildren; her mind, filled with romantic notions of the world, will misconstrue things. In terms of the narrative, Catherine's penchant for exaggerated language drawn from romance displays her dependency on Isabella for her taste and understanding. Eleanor Tilney, for her part, enjoys both romance and history. This displays her realism and common sense but also makes her somewhat literal-minded, as revealed in the conversation about the "horrors" in London discussed below.

Second, this discussion reflects Austen's insight about the connections between language, character, and insight. Language is the means by which we make sense of the world; if we are to have an accurate view of reality we must have accurate language. And seeing the world rightly is a central feature of good character. The Thorpes remake reality to their liking, but Henry insists on seeing reality as it is. Someone who has only one word (whether it be "nice" or "cool" or "awesome") that fits every situation is a person too lazy or too immature to see things and discriminate between them. If *everything* is nice, the word is robbed of all specific meaning. The fact that Catherine uses language in this manner is a sign of her immaturity, of her need to learn to see properly. Inform the ACLU: words must be discriminatory, applying to some things and not to others. Otherwise, all is smoothness.

Third, it is important that Henry is the teacher of the proper use of language. Though he is primarily a moral guide for Catherine, teaching her to speak accurately is part of her moral education. As a clergyman, Henry is fulfilling part of his pastoral role in connection with Catherine, for the church's role in society is to teach morals by teaching language and forming vocabulary.

Finally, Henry's discussion has implications for Austen's parody of the romance genre, for the exaggerated and imprecise language that Catherine uses is drawn from Gothic romance by way of Isabella. A further example of her dependence on romance for her language and view of things occurs later in the conversation when Catherine announces that "something very shocking indeed will soon come out in London," something "more horrible than anything we have met with yet" (p. 101). Eleanor is agitated, imagining that Catherine is talking about a "dreadful riot." Henry intervenes to clear up the confusion:

> "My dear Eleanor, the riot is only in your own brain. The confusion there is scandalous. Miss Morland has been talking of nothing more dreadful than a new publication which is shortly to come out, in three duodecimo volumes, two hundred and seventy-six pages in each, with a frontispiece to the first, of two tombstones and a lantern—do you understand? —And you, Miss Morland—my stupid sister has mistaken all your clearest expressions. You talked of expected horrors in London; and instead of instantly conceiving, as any rational creature would have done, that such words could relate only to a circulating library, she immediately pictured to herself a mob of three thousand men assembling in St. George's Fields; the Bank attacked, the Tower threatened, the streets of London flowing with blood, a detachment of the 12th Light Dragoons (the hopes of the nation) called up from Northampton to quell the insurgents, and the gallant Captain Frederick Tilney, in the moment of charging at the head of his troop, knocked off his horse by a brickbat from an upper window." (pp. 102–3)

On the surface, Henry is speaking for sanity and reality here. In contrast to the naive and impressionable Catherine, and what he calls his "simpleton" sister, Henry is the great exemplar of "proper artfulness." As Tave points out, Henry has skill in a variety of artistic endeavors: He can draw and has good taste in visual arts, he is able to explain to Catherine the "theory of the picturesque," and he dances well. He sees through the pretense and lies, and he can tell the difference between the shocking world of Gothic romance and the real world of England.

There is more than the surface here, however: underneath is a level of irony that not even Henry recognizes. St. George's Field, which he mentions in imagining a riot in London, was in fact the site of a riot in 1780, and Henry's description fits the facts of that riot quite closely. Though Henry is reassuring his sister and Catherine that there is no possibility of a riot in London, that the "horror" is just a figment of Catherine's Gothic imagination, he describes a scene that actually took place. This is not the last time that Henry will speak for realism and prove to be fundamentally *un*realistic. Perhaps Gothic romances are not so completely deceptive after all.

Review Questions

1. Explain how Austen parodies the Gothic romance at the beginning of her novel.

2. What kind of people are Isabella and John Thorpe?

3. Why does Catherine not see the Thorpes as they really are?

4. What kind of person is Henry Tilney?

5. Explain the significance of the conversation about language and literature during the Tilneys' outing with Catherine.

6. How does Austen show that Henry Tilney doesn't quite understand everything?

Thought Questions

1. In chapter one, Austen lists some snatches of poetry that Catherine learned. Where do these quotations come from? How are they important to the development of the story or the character of Catherine Morland?

2. Explain how Isabella Thorpe's language is an indicator of her character. Her conversation with Catherine in chapter six provides some good examples.

3. What kind of character is Mrs. Allen? Is she a suitable guardian for Catherine? Compare her as a guardian to other guardian figures in Austen's novels.

4. What is the point of John Thorpe's inquiry about Mr. Allen in chapter nine? How does this play out in the remainder of the book?

5. Discuss Henry Tilney's comparison of marriage and dance in chapter ten. How are they similar? What does Catherine think of the comparison?

6. It is raining in several scenes of part one. How is that significant to the development of the plot? Does it have any role in developing Austen's themes?

Part Two: Northanger Abbey

Many novels employ the device of a physical or geographic journey to depict a moral or spiritual journey. John Bunyan's *Pilgrim's Progress* uses this device in an openly allegoristic way, but many "realistic" novels use the same basic "allegory." Places have particular characteristics that present unique challenges and temptations to the hero. There are "vanity fairs" in Dickens (not to mention Thackeray) as much as in Bunyan. Catherine Morland's move from Bath to Northanger Abbey near the beginning of book two, therefore, represents a shift in theme, a new development in Catherine's growth, her "training for a heroine," and a new set of lessons to learn. Again, her teacher along the way is Henry Tilney, and she has enemies to contend with that are even more deceptive and vicious than the Thorpes.

As soon as she hears of Northanger Abbey, her expectations for adventure are aroused. Austen shifts back into the mode of parody: "Northanger Abbey!—These were thrilling words, and wound up Catherine's feelings to the highest point of ecstasy" (p. 124). On the dark and stormy first night of her stay, when she determines to investigate the contents of a mysterious chest in her room, she finds a handful of papers and is about to read them when her candle flickers and goes out:

A lamp could not have expired with more awful effect. Catherine, for a few moments, was motionless with horror. It was done completely; not a remnant of light in the wick could give hope to the rekindling breath. Darkness impenetrable and immovable filled the room. A violent gust of wind, rising with sudden fury, added fresh horror to the moment. Catherine trembled from head to foot. In the pause which succeeded, a sound like receding footsteps and the closing of a distant door struck on her affrighted ear. Human nature could support no more. A cold sweat stood on her forehead, the manuscript fell from her hand, and groping her way to the bed, she jumped hastily in, and sought some suspension of agony by creeping far underneath the clothes. (pp. 153–54)

Henry's story of Gothic adventures seems to be coming true, but in the morning, when she has the opportunity to examine the manuscript, she realizes she has found no more than a washing bill.

Catherine has perhaps made some progress in sensing the dynamics of character and relations, but she is still rather slow to draw accurate conclusions. Before she leaves for Northanger, she notices that Isabella, already engaged to James Morland, is paying a great deal of attention to Henry's brother, Captain Tilney:

It seemed to [Catherine] that Captain Tilney was falling in love with Isabella, and Isabella unconsciously encouraging him; unconsciously it must be, for Isabella's attachment to James was as certain and well acknowledged as her engagement. To doubt her truth or good intentions was impossible; and yet, during the whole of their conversation, her manner had been odd. She wished Isabella had talked more like her usual self, and not so much about money; and had not looked so well pleased at the sight of Captain Tilney. How strange that she should not perceive his admiration! Catherine longed to give her a hint of it, to put her on her guard, and prevent all the pain which her too lively behavior might otherwise create both for him and her brother. (pp. 131–132)

Of course, Isabella's encouragement is not unconscious in the least. Catherine senses something is amiss, but does not yet have an accurate sense of Isabella's character.

Her reaction to General Tilney is similar. She is astonished and gratified by his attention to her, but she is inexplicably uncomfortable with him and becomes aware that he brings discomfort to his children. And this leads her into ever wilder speculations about his marriage. She concludes from various hints that General Tilney had not loved his wife:

> Catherine attempted no longer to hide from herself the nature of the feelings which, in spite of all his attentions, he had previously excited; and what had been terror and dislike before was not absolute aversion. Yes, aversion! His cruelty to such a charming woman [as the deceased Mrs. Tilney] made him odious to her. She had often read of such characters; character which Mr. Allen had been used to call unnatural and overdrawn; but here was proof positive of the contrary. (p. 163)

From this, it is a small step for Catherine to conclude that General Tilney had murdered his wife.

Catherine's imaginary adventures come to a climax when she sneaks into a closed room at Northanger Abbey, expecting to find some evidence to support her theory. She is interrupted by Henry, who meets her on the landing and instantly understands her purpose in entering the room. His rebuke to Catherine is one of the key turning points in the story:

> "If I understand you rightly, you have formed a surmise of such horror as I have hardly words to—Dear Miss Morland, consider the dreadful nature of the suspicions you have entertained. What have you been judging from? Remember the country and the age in which we live. Remember that we are English, that we are Christians. Consult your own understanding, your own sense of the probable, your own observation of what is passing around you. Does our education prepare us for such atrocities? . . . Dearest Miss Morland, what ideas have you been admitting?" (p. 179)

Catherine goes out and begins to weep bitterly. This is one of the two great moral moments in Catherine Morland's life. The other occurs when she begins to see how despicable Isabella Thorpe is.

It is striking, and not accidental, that at this crucial moment in the Catherine development, Henry reminds her that she lives in a Christian country and that she is surrounded by Christians. In an important sense, this makes moral judgment far more difficult. If life were a Gothic romance, one could make moral judgments based on the gloominess of one's attic. But in the Christian country that is England, the good guys and bad guys are harder to discern, and sometimes villainy itself is not recognized as such. "The laws of the land, and the manners of the age" protect England from the most open forms of evil. Catherine draws this lesson immediately: Though there may be utter villains and complete angels on the Continent—"Italy, Switzerland, and the south of France"—yet "in England it was not so; among the English, she believed, in their hearts and habits, there was a general though unequal mixture of good and bad" (p. 181). This insight is still comically limited, since she leaves room for the possibility that Gothic romances realistically depict life elsewhere. Yet it is a genuine insight, and part of her education in the complexities of moral judgment and therefore of moral living.

Still, as in Henry's other speeches, there is a further level of irony here, for the Christian and orderly England that Henry invokes was not the England in which Jane Austen was living, something she was surely aware of. Spies, Jacobins, threats from the Continent were topics of daily conversation and newspaper coverage. And even within the fictional world of Northanger Abbey, not everyone acts by the standards of Christian charity. Even while disabusing Catherine of her fancies, Henry expresses an even more subtle fantasy—that the world is peaceful and orderly and all is light and good. Lionel Trilling got the point exactly right:

> We are quick, too quick, to understand that Northanger Abbey invites us into a snug conspiracy to disabuse the little heroine of

the errors of her corrupted fancy—Catherine Morland, having become addicted to novels of terror, has accepted their inadmissible premise, she believes that life is violent and unpredictable. And that is exactly what life is shown to be by the events of the story: it is we who must be disabused of our belief that life is sane and orderly.

As he did in the part one, Henry stands up for reason and realism, but Austen is subtly showing us that this is not the whole story. Horrible things do happen, even in such countries as England, even among people who think of themselves as Christians.

Henry is not even correct about his own father, who proves quite as much a monster as Catherine imagines. Catherine's expectations of horrors at *Northanger Abbey*, though exaggerated, are not completely off the mark. John Thorpe has been absent from the book for some time but his interference in Catherine's life continues to have its effects; in fact, it has the same effects in part two that it did in part one—separating Catherine from Henry. General Tilney's solicitous attitude toward Catherine has been largely based on a mistake, John Thorpe's lie that Catherine was heiress to the very wealthy Mr. Allen. When Catherine made it clear that she preferred Henry to John, John lied again, informing General Tilney that Catherine was in poverty. At that point, General Tilney removed her from the Abbey, complaining that *she* had deceived him. Though John Thorpe is certainly at fault here, General Tilney does not come off at all well; having been fooled once, he willingly allows himself to be fooled again. His own viciousness lies in his accepting the vicious lies of a vicious man.

When Henry informs his father about his intention to marry Catherine, General Tilney's rage is as black as anything Catherine had imagined:

> The general, accustomed on every ordinary occasion to give the law in his family, prepared for no reluctance but of feeling, no opposing desire that should dare to clothe itself in words, could ill brook the opposition of his son, steady as the sanction of reason and the dictate of conscience could make it. But, in such a

cause, his anger, though it must shock, could not intimidate Henry. . . . He steadily refused to accompany his father into Herefordshire, an engagement formed almost at the moment, to promote the dismissal of Catherine, and as steadily declared his intention of offering her his hand. The general was furious in his anger, and they parted in dreadful disagreement (p. 226).

The General's rage is eventually cooled, but his change of temper does not mark any improvement in his character. He is pacified only when Eleanor marries "a man of fortune and consequence," which "accession of dignity . . . threw him into a fit of good-humour till after Eleanor had obtained his forgiveness of Henry" (p. 228). At the end, General Tilney is as vicious a man as ever, a man clearly *capable* of killing his wife even if, in the event, he did not. As Brownstein points out, General Tilney has not killed his wife, but he is "insensitive, inhospitable, and selfish, obsessed with marrying his children for money," and she suggests that Catherine's instincts, formed as they were by Gothic romances, may have been "good guides to truth" after all. At least, it alerted her to the possibility that a dashing and strong-willed man like General Tilney might be inclined to abuse women, as he certainly does Catherine.

In the end, Gothic fiction is not so misleading as we might be led to believe. The "ideas" that it "admits" are valuable for shaping imagination, moral insight, and conduct. Austen's parody of Gothic, her apparently anti-novel novel, is most basically a defense of Gothic. Austen is too gleefully skeptical to believe the world is Gothic, but she apparently believed that confrontation with the imaginary demons of Gothic provides useful armor for confronting the more quotidian demons of the "Christian" world in the "central part of England."

Review Questions

1. What is significant about the geographic change at the beginning of book two?

2. What kind of man is General Tilney?

3. What does Catherine believe about General Tilney?

4. Explain the ironies of Henry's speech to Catherine in the stairs.

5. Why is Catherine forced to leave Northanger Abbey?

Thought Questions

1. What kind of person is Captain Tilney, Henry's brother? What does Henry think of his brother? Look especially at his conversation with Catherine in book two, chapter four.

2. Examine the passage about Henry's driving in book two, chapter five. To whom is Henry being contrasted? What does his driving say about his character?

3. What is the point of Henry's discussion of hyacinths in book two, chapter seven?

4. Who left the laundry list in the wardrobe at Northanger Abbey? How is this a further parody of romantic fiction?

5. What is Austen doing in the closing paragraph of the book? Is she saying that her book has no moral point to it? Or is she just *pretending* that the book has no moral point? If the latter, why does she say it?

CHAPTER 4

"I Conceal Nothing":
Sense and Sensibility

Sense and Sensibility centers on two sisters, Elinor and Marianne Dashwood. After the death of their father, they are forced to leave their home, Norland, when John Dashwood, their father's son by a previous marriage, inherits it and moves in. Elinor and Marianne move with their mother to Barton Cottage, near the home of Sir John and Lady Middleton. The novel traces the parallel romances of Elinor and Marianne, who both fall in love early in the novel, are betrayed by their lovers, and, of course, end happily married. Though the story concentrates fairly evenly on both sisters, Elinor is the primary heroine; the story is told from her perspective and her view of characters and events follows the narrator's. We know far more about Marianne than we do about Jane Bennet in *Pride and Prejudice*, but both are secondary heroines.

The book's title points to the main moral theme of the novel: Elinor represents "sense" and Marianne "sensibility." The latter is easier to notice and describe. As Austen uses the term, it refers to strong and sometimes ungoverned feeling, sensitivity to beauty in nature and art, impatience with the conventions and restraints of society. One of the key traits of sensibility is "openness," a willingness to express one's feelings freely without consideration for what is proper. "Sensibility" was not merely a moral issue but was characteristic of a certain kind of literature in Austen's time, sometimes described as "literature of sensibility." Many of the stories in this tradition describe the effects of excessive sensibility or emotion, where volcanic eruptions of excitement lead to hysteria and illness.

In her early work Austen often mocked this literature and pointed out the self-obsession that went along with it. One character in her teenage epistolary novel, "Love and Friendship," claims that "a sensibility too tremblingly alive to every affliction of my Friends, my Acquaintance and particularly to every affliction of my own, was my only fault, if a fault it could be called," and despises "that Inferior order of Beings with Regard to Delicate Feelings, tender Sentiments, and refined Sensibility." Characters of sensibility go into raptures over natural beauties, faint at the slightest breeze of affliction, and wallow in sorrow and regret.

One of Austen's earliest and most important insights about this literature is that its claim to naturalness and spontaneity is a deception. As Tave puts it,

> Transparently this kind of sensibility is, at every point, the reverse of what it claims to be. It sees and feels not more but less, because it is conventional, selfish, and weak. What is offered as natural and instinctive is a conduct learned from books and the product of a most elaborated art. The claim of freedom from ordinary social forms is resolved into a limited set of automatic responses. The claim of living by a higher law becomes actions according to a lower law. The vulnerability to suffering is not merely compensated by self-approval but overpaid by an imposition of the self upon others and a taking from them.

Most importantly for *Sense and Sensibility*, Austen shows that excessive sensibility collapses into mere selfishness, that people who oppose social norms and conventions in the name of feeling end up living the most conventional lives of all, and that people who claim to live out in the open are at least as secretive as everybody else.

Marianne displays all the traits of a heroine of sensibility and at times Austen treats her as an object of parody, much like Catherine Morland in *Northanger Abbey*. When her lover, Willoughby, leaves for a time, she plays the role of grieving lover to perfection:

Marianne would have thought herself very inexcusable had she been able to sleep at all on the first night after parting from Willoughby. She would have been ashamed to look her family in the face the next morning had she not risen from her bed in more need of repose than when she lay down on it. But the feelings which made such composure a disgrace, left her in no danger of incurring it. She was awake the whole night, and she wept the greatest part of it. She got up with an headache, was unable to talk, and unwilling to take any nourishment; giving pain every moment to her mother and sisters, and forbidden all attempt at consolation from either. Her sensibility was potent enough! . . .

The evening was passed off in the equal indulgence of feeling. She played over every favourite song that she had been used to play with Willoughby, every air in which their voices had been oftenest joined, and sat at the instrument gazing on every line of music that he had written out for her, till her heart was so heavy that no further sadness could be gained; and this nourishment of grief was every day applied. She spent whole hours at the pianoforte alternately singing and crying, her voice often totally suspended by her tears. In books, too, as well as in music, she courted the misery which a contrast between the past and present was certain of giving. She read nothing but what they had been used to read together. (p. 60)[†]

Austen's description indicates that Marianne's passion has a self-conscious quality to it: She knows how lovers are supposed to act when they are separated, and so she is determined to act that way. Because she indulges and allows free rein to her sensibility, she becomes heedless of the pain it causes her mother and sisters. This description also makes it obvious that Austen knew that violent passion was a *learned* behavior, not a natural mode of expression.

Marianne's reaction to falling leaves is also typical of this parody:

"Oh!" cried Marianne, "with what transporting sensations have I formerly seen them fall! How have I delighted, as I walked, to see them driven in showers about me by the wind! What feelings have they, the season, the air altogether inspired! Now there is no

---

[†] Page numbers in this chapter are taken from the paperback Modern Library edition (2001), with an introduction by David Gates.

one to regard them. They are seen only as a nuisance, swept hastily off, and driven as much as possible from the sight." (p. 63)

Echoing the irony of the narrator, Elinor comments wryly that "It is not everyone . . . who has your passion for dead leaves" (p. 63). In Marianne's speech, as elsewhere in Austen's novels, syntax—the way something is said—is a key indicator of character. The abundance of exclamation points, the explicit references to her own feelings and the exaggerated way she describes them, and the links with tumultuous natural phenomenon (driven in showers by the wind) all point to her lack of restraint. Like all romantics, Marianne finds particular delight in feelings of regret, loss, and pain: she loves *dead* leaves.

Yet for all that, Marianne is not simply a parody of the heroine of novels of sensibility. For many readers she is far more vivid and attractive than her sister Elinor, who, as noted above, is structurally the central character in the book. Far more than Catherine Morland, Marianne comes alive as a character in her own right, and the description of her anguish at the loss of Willoughby is not ironic and detached. Elinor enters Marianne's room to find her

> stretched out on the bed, almost choked by grief, one letter in her hand, and two or three others lying by her. Elinor drew near, but without saying a word; and seating herself on the bed, took her hand, kissed her affectionately several times, and then gave way to a burst of tears, which at first was scarcely less violent than Marianne's. The latter, though unable to speak, seem to feel all the tenderness of this behaviour, and after some time thus spend in joint affliction, she put all the letters into Elinor's hands; and then covering her face with her handkerchief, almost screamed with agony. (p. 128)

Few passages in Austen's novels are as straightforwardly passionate as this. There is not a hint of irony; Austen, like Elinor, is all sympathy. Even here, though, Marianne's feelings are not beyond criticism. She has been at a peak of violent emotion so often that it is difficult for her to find a higher emotional register when she is really distressed, and it is also hard for readers to believe that she is really suffering quite as intensely as she appears to be.

In this scene, Elinor displays an important dimension of "sensibility," and this point is crucial to understanding Austen's treatment. In response to the individualistic ideas of human nature and the idea that man was innately selfish, many writers of the eighteenth century claimed that sympathy is the most characteristic feature of human existence. Adam Smith, who is seen as a founding father of economics for his *Wealth of Nations*, also wrote a treatise on the *Theory of Moral Sentiments*. According to Smith and other writers of his time, men are not inherently selfish and unsociable, but sociable and sympathetic, and the moral life arises not from a pursuit of self-interest but from sympathy, "feeling-with" others. Elinor feels Marianne's anguish and feels it with almost equal intensity. One of the ironies of Austen's book is that Marianne's intense sensibility (her feelings) sometimes undermines her sensibility (her sympathy with others). Excessive sensibility, Austen shows, is often nothing more than egotism.

Elinor's sympathy with Marianne indicates that she possesses true sensibility, which Tave describes as "a feeling recognition of the rightful claims of others and of one's own responsibilities." It is the opposite of selfishness or egotism and thus true and false sensibility, though similar on the surface, are, morally speaking, polar opposites. True sensibility is associated with "candor." In Austen's time, the word did not refer to open and frank discourse ("give me your candid opinion of this lime green tie"). Rather, candor meant charity in judgment—trying to put the best construction on everything. In this too, true sensibility is the opposite of its false imitator: False sensibility judges others harshly; true sensibility judges with kindness.

Overall, Elinor is the representative of the other pole of Austen's title, "sense." Austen's initial description of Elinor's character indicates some features of this virtue:

> Elinor, the eldest daughter whose advice was so effectual, possessed a strength of understanding, and coolness of judgment,

which qualified her, though only nineteen, to be the counsellor of her mother, and enabled her frequently to counteract, to the advantage of them all, that eagerness of mind in Mrs. Dashwood which must generally have led to imprudence. She had an excellent heart; her disposition was affectionate, and her feelings were strong: but she knew how to govern them: it was a knowledge which her mother had yet to learn, and which one of her sisters had resolved never to be taught. (p. 5)

Elinor's sense is displayed in her knowledge and mature judgment, which help to restrain both her sister and her mother. This description makes clear that sense is not the absence of feeling but rather the government of feeling; and this government is partly a response to the needs and demands of others. In this respect sense is necessarily allied with true sensibility; acting sensibly means recognizing the claims that others have on us. True sensibility means recognizing that we are not our own.

Other characters in the novel can generally be lined up along this spectrum of sense and sensibility. Willoughby is clearly a male Marianne, all sensibility and little sense. The other male characters, Edward Ferrars and Colonel Brandon, are more characters of sense, though neither is very striking. Brandon is older, grave, reserved, of a disposition exactly the opposite of Willoughby's. Elinor recognizes that while "a general resemblance of disposition between the parties might forward the affection of Mr. Willoughby, an equally striking opposition of character was no hindrance to the regard of Colonel Brandon" (p. 36). Edward has moderate ambitions and is not exuberant in any way, exhibiting, as John Lauber points out, a tongue-tied embarrassment more frequently than any other emotion.

In other ways, the novel has a very symmetrical structure, with pairs and triads everywhere. Two Mr. Dashwoods are mentioned at the beginning of the novel, and both die. Aside from the Dashwoods, there are two other pairs of sisters: Lady Middleton and Mrs. Palmer, and Lucy and Nancy Steele. There are two families with spoiled and unbearable children: the Middletons and the Palmers. Turns in the plot come in pairs as well: There are two secret engagements, or rather, one that is believed to be a secret engagement (and is not), and another that is not known at all, but is actually a secret engagement. There are two attachments broken, and they are broken for similar reasons: Elinor thinks that her hopes for Edward are over when she learns of his secret engagement, and Marianne knows that Willoughby is gone when she learns of his engagement to the wealthy Miss Grey. David Gates points out other balancing plot points:

> Two scenes with telltale locks of hair. Two scenes in which approaching horsemen are misidentified. Two hasty departures to London on secret "business." Two young men (dependent on two rich and bossy old ladies) who dally unjustifiably with two sisters. Two illegitimate daughters of two Elizas.

All this might suggest that Austen has written a novel with a geometry text as her guide, in order to provide a simple "binary" contrast of sense and sensibility and, no doubt, in order to advocate the superiority of sense. We have already seen enough of the complexity of the two terms in the title to know that any simple contrast of the two is impossible, and much of the novel is an exploration of the complexities of the interplay between strong emotion, sympathy for others, and common sense.

A further sign of these complexities emerges when we consider the issue of "secrets" in the novel. Theoretically, it would appear that characters of sensibility have no secrets; they wear their feelings on their sleeves and express them to everyone in every circumstance. Yet everyone believes that Marianne and Willoughby, the two most passionate characters in the novel, are secretly engaged, and this supposed secret is the occasion for much speculation in the first half of the book. But it is not only the characters of sensibility who have secrets. Secrecy is pervasive in *Sense and Sensibility*: Elinor has to keep the secret that Lucy has revealed to her, and also to keep secret the pain it causes her; Brandon keeps a secret about his relationship with Eliza, and consequently her relationship with Willoughby; Edward keeps the secret about his engagement with Lucy.

With so many secrets, finding out what really is going on is a considerable challenge, and this makes it difficult to form fitting judgments about people and situations. To quote Gates again: "During most of *Sense and Sensibility* . . . characters get their information in what, for Austen, is the normal way: that is, through spying, eavesdropping, and accidental overhearing; through rumor, gossip, and inference; through incomplete, misleading, or downright false communication." But the other challenge is knowing what to keep secret and what to reveal. Both sense and sensibility are required if the flow of information is going to be controlled.

We can illustrate this by imagining a world without secrets. Suppose that your every thought and desire were instantly made public, along with the thoughts and desires of all your neighbors. Suppose that everything that was whispered in your ear was immediately shouted from the housetops. It does not take much imagination to conclude that such a world is simply unbearable. Even if we were not wretched sinners, no one would want to live under that kind of scrutiny. Since we *are* sinners, our horror at the idea of being completely transparent to the world is increased to a nearly infinite degree. People commonly kill themselves rather than face the horror of exposure. Secrecy is simply an essential feature of human social life, and Austen sees that one of the virtues of a code of manners and propriety is that it keeps secrets properly concealed.

At the same time, complete secrecy is equally damaging. If I know that your neighbor molests children, I am harming you if I avert my eyes when I see your children playing at his house. Some things that are whispered in the ear *must* be shouted on the housetops. If everything is kept secret, then the only reasonable way to live is to distrust everybody. Unless I can assume that murderers are going to be exposed, child molesters prosecuted, snipers caught, it would be reasonable for me to assume that everyone I see is a murderer, a child molester, or a sniper. Balancing concealment and exposure is one of the trickiest problems in personal relations and in social life at large. Break a confidence and you lose a friend; keep a friend's secret that should be exposed and you harm a friend.

In *Sense and Sensibility*, some keep things secret that should be made public; others, for various reasons, make things public that should be kept secret; at other times, secrets lurk in the corners of social life causing embarrassment, pain, and confusion; at still other times, the secret knowledge that secrets are known to others has the same effect. Only characters who combine sense and sensibility in proper proportion conceal what should be concealed and reveal what should be revealed.

One final element in this cluster of themes may be mentioned. Among the most intimate of secrets are one's feelings and emotions, especially feelings of love and romantic or sexual desire. These are also among the most volatile of human emotions. In the secrecy of his heart, a man can fall in love and out of love ten times a day, and that is just on the way to the office. Again, imagine a world in which a man acted on each of those desires; families would be in a far greater mess than they actually are. Sexual desires cannot be made public in this kind of immediate way without destroying society. It is essential, then, that sexual desires be regulated by some kind of institutional structures.

One of the great failings of characters of sensibility is the damage they cause by refusing to accept the public and institutional regulation of their emotions. In this way, again, Austen proves herself a perceptive social commentator, showing the virtues of institutional structures by showing the evils that come from flouting them.

Review Questions

1. What is "sensibility"?

2. How does Marianne display sensibility? How does Austen show the limits of her sensibility?

3. Is Marianne a parody of the "heroine of sensibility"? Why or why not?

4. What is "sense"? How does Elinor display it?

5. Discuss the "binary" structure of the novel.

6. Explain how the male characters line up on the spectrum of sense-sensibility.

7. Discuss the prominence of the issue of secrecy in *Sense and Sensibility*.

8. Why is secrecy necessary to human life? Why must secrecy be limited?

Book One (Chapters 1–22)

John and Fanny Dashwood are characters dominated by sense. John is the stepson of Mrs. Dashwood, stepbrother to Marianne and Elinor, and Fanny, his wife, is Edward Ferrars's sister. The narrator initially describes him as a "steady, respectable character," whose lack of sensibility is seen in the absence of "the strong feelings of the rest of his family." Austen caustically comments, "He was not ill-disposed, unless to be rather coldhearted, and rather selfish, is to be ill-disposed." Fanny, for her part, is described in equally harsh terms as a "strong caricature of himself; more narrow-minded and selfish" (p. 4). Full of sense but lacking sensibility, John and Fanny are simply selfish, and their sense is really a cover for self-interest. At the extremes, selfish sense and selfish sensibility kiss each other.

The conversation of John and Fanny in chapter two traces the development of sense into selfishness into cruelty. Though he had promised his father that he would care for the Dashwood girls, John's weak family sympathies are overwhelmed by Fanny's "irresistible" argument. Initially, John intends to provide 3000 pounds for the Dashwoods, but that figure is gradually negotiated down to occasional gifts of some fifty pounds. By the end of the conversation, John is speculating about *taking* china from the Dashwoods: "some of the plate would have been a very pleasant addition to our own stock here" (p. 10). Fanny could not agree more: The Dashwood's china is "a great deal too handsome, in my opinion, for any place *they* can ever afford to live in" (p. 10). Detached from sensibility, and the sympathy associated with it, sense turns into larceny. One of the most striking, and horrifying, things about the scene is the utter reasonableness of it all; John and Fanny seem perfectly respectable and even congratulate themselves on their generosity, all the while plotting to rob widows and evict orphans.

John Dashwood's sense turns not only into cruelty but into senselessness. He consistently misunderstands characters and situations, and therefore forms mistaken expectations about what will happen. His concern that giving money to the Dashwoods would harm his son's fortunes is ludicrous; John and Fanny are so wealthy that the impact of assisting Mrs. Dashwood would be minimal. He is equally mistaken about characters. When he has met Lady Middleton and Mrs. Jennings, he cannot wait to tell Fanny about them: "Lady Middleton is really a most elegant woman! Such a woman as I am sure Fanny will be glad to know. And Mrs. Jennings too, an exceedingly well-behaved woman, though not so elegant as her daughter" (pp. 161–2). By this time, we have already known Lady Middleton and Mrs. Jennings for some while, and know that their true character has very little to do with John's description.

Standing in contrast to John Dashwood, Elinor is the spokeswoman for proper sense, sense allied to sensibility. Yet, she too is often mistaken in her analysis of situations. Marianne's "engagement" to Willoughby is a key example. After Willoughby leaves for the first time, Elinor discusses with her mother the possibility that Marianne and Willoughby are engaged. Mrs. Dashwood is certain that they are, but refuses to inquire. Initially, Elinor says that "every circumstance except *one* is in favour of their engagement, but that *one* is the total silence of both on the subject, and with me it almost outweighs every other." But she decides that "If we find they correspond, every fear of mine will be removed" (p. 58). They do correspond, and Elinor concludes they are engaged. She observes a conversation between Willoughby and Marianne, whose intimacy leaves her with no doubt about their engagement. She is wrong in both instances.

Later, she is wrong about the source of Edward's melancholy:

She placed all that was astonishing in this way of acting to his mother's account; and it was happy for her that he had a mother whose character was so imperfectly known to her, as to be the general excuse for everything strange on the part of her son. . . . His want of spirits, of openness, and of consistency, were most usually attributed to his want of independence, and his better knowledge of Mrs. Ferrars's dispositions and designs. . . . She would have been glad to know when these difficulties were to cease, this opposition was to yield—when Mrs. Ferrars would be reformed, and her son be at liberty to be happy. (pp. 72–73)

As she later discovers, Edward's melancholy arises instead from the fact that he is secretly and unhappily engaged to Lucy Steele. Elinor's two errors are ironically related: On the one hand, she wrongly believes that Willoughby and Marianne are secretly engaged, while on the other hand she wrongly attributes Edward's melancholy, which is the result of a secret engagement, to another source. At least Elinor recognizes this limitation: "I have frequently detected myself in such kind of mistakes . . . in a total misapprehension of character in some point or other" (p.). This self-criticism is part of her sense.

Characters associated with sensibility also make errors of judgment, but lack the self-critical insight of Elinor. Even before Willoughby has appeared, Marianne is speculating about Elinor's future with Edward: "No sooner did she perceive any symptom of love in his behaviour to Elinor, than she considered their serious attachment as certain, and looked forward to their marriage as rapidly approaching" (p. 13). Confidently, she tells her mother that Elinor will be "settled for life" in "a few months" (p. 13).

Marianne's and Elinor's mistakes in analyzing situations, evaluating character, and predicting outcomes are understandable given the pervasive secrecy that characterizes the society of the novel. Secrecy is forced on the characters in part by the demand for decorum and proper manners. When the code of manners trains people to act and speak in certain ways, they necessarily suppress and hide certain feelings and desires. A young man might be intensely attracted to a young woman, but if the code forbids him to speak to her privately, he has to keep those feelings to himself. This is the kind of secrecy that is inherent to and necessary to any ordered social life.

Elinor is a specialist in this proper mode of secrecy. She keeps a number of secrets during the novel, particularly the secret of Lucy's engagement with Edward. Marianne, on the other hand, claims to hide nothing; she is a woman who has no secrets. While they are visiting London later in the novel, Marianne is disappointed that she has not received a letter from Willoughby. Elinor asks if she is expecting a letter. Marianne is evasive, and Elinor says that "you have no confidence in me, Marianne." Marianne responds with "Nay, Elinor, this reproach from *you*! You have confidence in no one!" When Elinor protests that she has nothing to tell, Marianne responds, "Nor I . . . our situations then are alike. We have neither of us anything to tell; you, because you communicate, and I, because I conceal nothing" (p. 119).

This is not in fact the case, since the exact nature of Marianne's relationship with Willoughby is kept secret during the first part of the novel. But the secrecy of Marianne and Willoughby has a very different source from the secrecy of Elinor. Instead of being a means for preserving social life, their secrecy is part of a conscious assault on the conventions of society, an assault that extends to nearly every area of life. In language, Marianne abhors "every commonplace phrase by which wit is intended" (p. 33): She mocks Brandon and Edward for their self-restraint, and she explicitly condemns Elinor for keeping secrets. From his first appearance, Willoughby acts on the impulse or necessity of the moment, without much regard to proprieties. When he rescues Marianne from her fall, he picks her up and carries her to the house, thinking only that "her modesty declined what her situation rendered necessary" (p. 31). And he barges into Barton Cottage with Marianne in his arms, much to the amazement of Elinor and Mrs. Dashwood, and deposits her in a chair in the parlor. Later, Willoughby gives Marianne a horse, which Marianne accepts without thinking of the cost to her mother. Both, in this case, act without thinking of any inconvenience of impropriety that could follow.

Austen summarizes their attitude toward control of emotions or intimacy in a concise paragraph:

> Marianne abhorred all concealment where no real disgrace could attend unreserve; and to aim at the restraint of sentiments which were not in themselves illaudable, appeared to her not merely an unnecessary effort, but a disgraceful subjection of reason to commonplace and mistaken notions. Willoughby thought the same; and their behaviour, at all times, was an illustration of their opinions. (p. 39)

For Marianne, things should be concealed only when revealing them would bring "real disgrace." Whether any good comes from the exposure is not important. It is also significant that this paragraph summarizes Marianne's attitudes fully, but says only that "Willoughby thought the same," a subtle indication that Marianne's voracious sensibility controls their relationship. She has found the kind of man she desired, one whose every taste corresponds exactly to her own.

Like other characters of sensibility, Marianne and Willoughby think of themselves as members of a superior race. Marianne is harsh in her criticisms of Edward's lack of passion, and Willoughby and Marianne join in merry ridicule of Brandon. In this sense too, Marianne's self-conscious and cultivated passion undermines true sensibility.

Keeping the true nature of their relationship concealed is a sign of their impatience with "commonplace" notions. The respectable thing to do would be for Willoughby to make his intentions explicit to Mrs. Dashwood. The "commonplace" approach would be to make the engagement, if there is one, public; and, if there is no engagement, to avoid behavior that suggests otherwise. In short, the commonplace approach to courtship is to expose it, and not to conceal it. And this exposure, far from causing damage or scandal, would be a protection for Marianne. Had the relationship with Marianne been more officially formalized, Willoughby would have not been able to pursue another woman so readily; the potential scandal of breaking an engagement would have inhibited (if not prevented) him from abandoning Marianne. So long as their relationship remained formlessly unofficial, he is free to come and go as he pleases. Tony Tanner puts the point well:

> What Elinor wants is that Marianne's love affair should be brought out of the formlessness of feeling into the defining forms of society. Otherwise she fears it might have no real continuity—and in the event she is right, though we cannot by the same token say that Marianne is wrong.

What characterizes Willoughby and Marianne is not so much complete openness as openness about things that should be concealed and openness where concealment is required.

The issue of secrecy also helps to explain something of the flatness of the other male characters in the story. Brandon is certainly not without affection and sensibility. Even Marianne appreciates his quiet responsiveness to her piano playing. His taste is made particularly evident by the contrast with other characters. Sir John goes into raptures without understanding and without taste, and will not even stop his praise long enough to listen. Lady Middleton hushes her husband, but is so inattentive that she asks Marianne to sing a song she has just finished. Some react to Marianne's music with loud expressions of pleasure, and some with quiet inattention. Colonel Brandon represents a third reaction, a real enjoyment without the effusive raptures that Marianne herself would have exhibited.

Despite his real feeling, however, Brandon is a grave and quiet man, who speaks little and who often, when he does speak, has difficulty finishing sentences. During one conversation with Elinor about Marianne's belief that "second attachments" cannot exist, Brandon makes this incoherent comment:

> "This," said he, "cannot hold; but a change, a total change of sentiments— No, no, do not desire it, for when the romantic refinements of a young mind are obliged to give way, how frequently are they succeeded by such opinions as are too common,

and too dangerous! I speak from experience. I once knew a lady who in temper and mind greatly resembled your sister, who thought and judged like her, but who from an enforced change—from a series of unfortunate circumstances—" Here he stopped suddenly. (p. 41)

Whatever is he talking about? At this point, we do not know, but we later find that Brandon's hesitations, the fits and starts of his conversation, are not the product of a lack of intelligence or feeling, but rather are the product of a secret past that he must suppress.

Edward is under similar constraints and it shows in his speech and demeanor. In fact, during the initial chapters where Elinor and Edward are getting acquainted, we never hear him speak at all. Marianne discusses him with Mrs. Dashwood and probes Elinor for clues about her feelings, but Edward says not a word. When he visits the Dashwoods at Barton Cottage (chap. sixteen), he is allowed to speak a few lines, but says nothing of moment or wit. Struck by his "coldness and reserve," Elinor goes away from the encounter "mortified . . . vexed and half angry" (p. 64). Like Brandon, Edward's reticence is the product of secrecy.

In a world of secrets, the exposer of secrets has a unique power. Among the characters in the book, no one is so thoroughly a hunter of secrets as Mrs. Jennings, Lady Middleton's mother. When Margaret, the youngest Dashwood daughter, reveals to Mrs. Jennings that Elinor has a lover whose name begins with "F," Mrs. Jennings cannot rest until she has broken the code. This is only one illustration of her main gift and purpose in life:

> She had only two daughters, both of whom she had lived to see respectably married, and she had now therefore nothing to do but to marry all the rest of the world. In the promotion of this object, she was zealously active, as far as her ability reached, and missed no opportunity of projecting weddings among all the young people of her acquaintance. She was remarkably quick in the discovery of attachments, and had enjoyed the advantage of raising blushes and the vanity of many a young woman by insinuations of her power over such a young man; and this kind of

discernment enabled her soon after her arrival at Barton, deci-
sively to pronounce that Colonel Brandon was very much in love
with Marianne Dashwood. (pp. 26–27)

Her whole agenda is to open up secrets, to expose secret alliances.

Mrs. Jennings wants to uncover secrets but she lacks sense
enough to decipher the clues that are before her. After Brandon
leaves abruptly, abandoning a planned outing, Mrs. Jennings speculates on the causes:

> The sudden termination of Colonel Brandon's visit at the Park,
> with his steadiness in concealing its cause, filled the mind and
> raised the wonder of Mrs. Jennings for two or three days: she was
> a great wonderer, as everyone must be who takes a very lively
> interest in all the comings and goings of all their acquaintances.
> She wondered with little intermission what could be the reason
> of it; was sure that there must be some bad news, and thought
> over every kind of distress that could have befallen him, with a
> fixed determination that he should not escape them all. . . . So
> wondered, so talked Mrs. Jennings; her opinions varying with
> every fresh conjecture, and all seeming equally probably as they
> arose. (pp. 50–51)

The whole Middleton family represents the extremes of sense
and sensibility. Sir John is as interested in exposing Elinor's secrets
as Mrs. Jennings, and he usually tells them quite openly. He tells
everyone that Elinor's lover is named Ferrars "in a very audible
whisper" but goes on to say, "but pray do not tell it, for it's a great
secret." His chief interest, however, is hunting. Everything and
everyone is judged in relation to this obsession. When asked about
Willoughby's character, he can only say "As good a kind of fellow
as ever lived, I assure you. A very decent shot, and there is not a
bolder rider in England," or, when pressed, "he is a pleasant, good-
humoured fellow, and has the nicest little black bitch of a pointer
I ever saw" (p. 32). Lady Middleton is "a mother" who shows
hospitality only to display her elegance, and whose only enjoyment comes from her "four noisy children" who rush in after

dinner to pull her, tear her clothes, and "put an end to every kind of discourse except what directly related to themselves" (pp. 24, 25).

Sir John is a grotesque parody of sensibility, while Lady Middleton, with her "cold insipidity," is a parody of sense. The latter point is highlighted much later in the book when Lady Middleton and Fanny meet for the first time: Fanny finds Lady Middleton "one of the most charming women in the world!" and Lady Middleton "was equally pleased with Mrs. Dashwood. There was a kind of coldhearted selfishness on both sides, which mutually attracted them; and they sympathised with each other in an insipid propriety of demeanor, and a general want of understanding" (p. 162). Mrs. Jennings' other family, the Palmers, are the reverse; Mr. Palmer is sullen and uncommunicative, obviously embarrassed by his idiotic wife, while his wife laughs inappropriately at her husband's behavior and generally makes a fool of herself. At times, the company of these people becomes unbearable, especially to Marianne. Austen's depiction of the realities of common social life is more harshly satirical in *Sense and Sensibility* than in any other novel. John Lauber suggests that the book leaves the impression that neither sense nor sensibility is a common trait.

Mrs. Jennings' good-natured detective work is played for comic effect. For all her vulgarity, she is a good-hearted and decent woman. The same cannot be said for another character who reveals secrets, Lucy Steele. Despite her smart dress and civil manners, Lucy's lack of "elegance and artlessness" is immediately evident to Elinor. Not that Lucy is without intelligence; she is a perfect embodiment of the same kind of sense that drives John and Fanny Dashwood, the sense that pursues self-interest above all. One of her main strategies for pursuing her interest is to reveal secrets. She tells Elinor of her secret engagement to Edward to hurt Elinor and to dash any hopes she has for him. At the end of book one, we leave Elinor thinking and feeling miserable.

Review Questions

1. How do the various characters line up on the spectrum of sense and sensibility?

2. How are John and Fanny Dashwood parodies of sense?

3. Discuss the limitations of Elinor's judgment about characters and situations. Why is she so often mistaken?

4. How do Elinor and Marianne differ with regard to "concealment"? What do they conceal and why?

5. What role does Mrs. Jennings play with regard to the theme of secrecy?

6. Describe the characters of the Middletons.

7. What kind of person is Lucy Steele? How does she use secrets?

Thought Questions

1. What are the different characters' attitudes toward the arts of music and drawing? How does this help to establish their characters?

2. Why does Austen continually depict children as small ogres? How does it relate to her criticism of extreme sensibility?

3. Discuss the episodes with the locks of hair. How does this relate to the larger themes of the book?

4. Why does Willoughby leave for London and what happens while he is there? To answer this question, you will need to read further and put some pieces together.

5. In several scenes, Marianne is expecting someone to arrive, and another man comes instead. What is the purpose of these scenes?

Books Two–Three

Book one ended with both Elinor's and Marianne's "beaux" absent. Willoughby has mysteriously gone to London and Edward has made only a bit appearance since the opening chapters.

At the end of book one, Elinor's hopes for marriage to Edward have been dashed by the revelation that he is already engaged, and a similar event will soon dash Marianne's hopes for Willoughby. Visiting London in the company of Mrs. Jennings, Marianne every day expects some news or visit from Willoughby. Though his card is left, he never appears, until they unexpectedly encounter him at a ball. Willoughby is formal and avoids directly looking at Marianne. When asked if he had received her letters, he replies stiffly, "Yes, I had the pleasure of receiving the information of your arrival in town, which you were so good as to send me," and then "turned hastily away with a slight bow and joined his [woman] friend" (p. 124). Suddenly Willoughby, who has been the one voluble male character in the novel, has become tongue-tied as the other men. And for the same reason: Now he too has a secret which he hopes to conceal from the Dashwood sisters. Soon after, Willoughby writes a viciously impassive letter breaking off all his attachment to Marianne. They soon receive the news that Willoughby has been engaged to a wealthy Miss Grey.

Shortly into book two, the two sisters are in precisely the same situation: Both have been suspected (wrongly) of being engaged, and now both have seen their hopes destroyed because of their lovers' engagements to other women. Though they are in similar situations, however, their reactions are sharply opposed. Passionate as always, Marianne throws herself into hysterics of grief and later becomes seriously ill while walking toward Willoughby's home. Two conversations especially highlight the differences of their reactions. In the first conversation, Marianne refuses the comfort that Elinor provides and implies that Elinor, whom she thinks is secure in her love for Edward, cannot understand her pain:

> "Exert yourself, dear Marianne," [Elinor] cried, "if you would not kill yourself and all who love you. Think of your mother; think of her misery while *you* suffer; for her sake you must exert yourself."
>
> "I cannot, I cannot," cried Marianne; "leave me, leave me, if I distress you; leave me, hate me, forget me; but do not torture me

so. Oh! How easy for those who have no sorrow of their own to talk of exertion! Happy, happy Elinor, *you* cannot have an idea of what I suffer."

"Do not call *me* happy, Marianne! Ah; if you knew! And can you believe me to be so while I see you so wretched!"

"Forgive me, forgive me," throwing her arms round her sister's neck; "I know you feel for me; I know what a heart you have; but yet you are—you must be happy; Edward loves you—what, oh! what can do away such happiness as that!"

"Many, many circumstances," said Elinor solemnly.

"No, no, no," cried Marianne wildly; "he loves you, and only you. You *can* have no grief." (p. 130)

Marianne's suffering is so all-consuming and all-embracing that she leaves no room for anyone else to suffer, and she has no patience with anyone else's claims. Nowhere in the novel does the essential selfishness of Marianne's sensibility stand out so starkly.

The other conversation is first reported indirectly. Once Edward's engagement is made public, Elinor finds that she must tell Marianne what she knows:

Her narration was clear and simple; and though it could not be given without emotion, it was not accompanied by violent agitation nor impetuous grief. *That* belonged rather to the hearer, for Marianne listened with horror, and cried excessively. Elinor was to be the comforter of others in her own distresses no less than in theirs. (p. 183)

While the earlier conversation revealed the selfishness of Marianne's grief, this conversation shows the unselfishness of Elinor's sense. The lesson is not lost on Marianne:

"Four months! Have you known of this four months?"
Elinor confirmed it.
"What! while attending to me in all my misery, has this been on your heart? and I have reproached you for being happy!"
"It was not fit that you should then know how much I was the reverse."

"Four months!" cried Marianne again. "So calm! so cheerful! How have you been supported?"

"By feeling that I was doing my duty." (p. 184)

When Marianne expresses once again her astonishment that Elinor could have kept her secret so long despite her love for Edward, Elinor explains further: "Yes. But I did not love only him; and while the comfort of others was dear to me, I was glad to spare them from knowing how much I felt" (p. 184). Elinor's sense is revealed here as a specifically Christian virtue; she does not subordinate her passions, in Stoic fashion, to her reason. Rather, she governs her passions so that she can do her duty; she subordinates her passion for the sake of love and self-sacrifice.

If book one was about concealment, books two–three are about secrets revealed, a theme anticipated by Lucy's revelations at the end of book one. We readers have known of Elinor's secret for some time, but that is revealed to Marianne for the first time. Far and away the most dramatic revelation, however, is Brandon's revelation of Willoughby's villainy toward Brandon's niece, Eliza, whom Willoughby had seduced, and left pregnant, poor, and abandoned (chap. thirty-one). In the process, Brandon also reveals his own secret, the secret of his rapid departure to London, which was in response to a letter informing him that Eliza had been found after being missing for eight months. In all this, Brandon proves himself, by Austen's standards, an admirable mixture of sense and sensibility. Like a man of sense, he withheld damaging information when it could do no good, but, out of sympathy for Marianne's grief, he informed Elinor. Unlike Lucy Steele, who reveals secrets to cause pain, Brandon reveals secrets to relieve pain.

Willoughby's final situation is an ironic inversion of his original outlook. He burst into the story as a free spirit, a romantic hero who flouted convention and went his own way. When push came to shove, however, he chooses wealth and status over love; the most openly unconventional character bows to convention. Rather surprisingly, however, Austen is not done with Willoughby. Just when Elinor has concluded that he is an utter villain, he shows up at night energetically to confess his wrong and to give an account of his behavior. He is not fully exonerated. Elinor concludes that from start to finish he had acted only out of self-ishness; and she recognizes in him a parable of

> the irreparable injury which too early an independence and its consequent habits of idleness, dissipation, and luxury, have made in the mind, the character, the happiness, of a man who, to every advantage of person and talents, united a disposition naturally open and honest, and a feeling, affectionate temper. The world had made him extravagant and vain; extravagance and vanity had made him cold-hearted and selfish. Vanity . . . had involved him in a real attachment, which extravagance, or at least its offspring necessity, had required to be sacrificed. (p. 234)

Despite this sharp and accurate judgment on Willoughby's character, Elinor does abandon her conclusion that he had descended into utter villainy. As Willoughby leaves, she offers her hand with the assurance that his explanation removes "a little" of his guilt.

Despite this, and despite Willoughby's charm, energy, and "manly beauty," in the end he suffers by comparison with the other men. Throughout the book, Brandon is a careful and responsible man, but one who has deep feelings for Marianne. Edward is even more directly contrasted with Willoughby. The latter abandoned Marianne when he realized that he was in danger of losing his inheritance; faced with the wrath of his cousin and benefactor, Mrs. Smith, he finds a rich fiancée rather than risk poverty. Faced with his mother's threat of disinheritance, by contrast, Edward determined to remain in an engagement that had long before lost its charm. Willoughby was a great professor of romantic love, but he marries for money, while Brandon and Edward marry for love. Willoughby might seem to be the dashing and courageous one. Edward's explanation of his dithering behavior is not satisfying, but still he shows strength that Willoughby does not. By comparison with Edward, Willoughby is a wimp.

For those who have been following Austen with care, this should not be a surprise. His retreat to sheer hardheaded calculation, his retreat to "sense," is really not surprising. His sensibility always was a calculated affair, always guided by conventions of what the books said lovers and romantics should say and do. In fact, Willoughby never emerged as a man at all, even from the beginning. Sure, he has his "black bitch" and his gun and his hat and his "manly beauty"—all the apparatus of manhood, as Austen might have said. What he lacks is manhood itself. He never displays the self-confidence to be *different* from Marianne, whose tastes and passions completely dominate him. How likely is it, after all, that Marianne would stumble (pun intended) on a young man with *precisely* the same musical, literary, and poetic tastes as herself? She made him into an image of herself, and when he takes up with Miss Grey, she "forces" him to write a cruel letter to Marianne. Bland and colorless as Edward and Brandon sometimes appear, at least they never allow themselves to be reduced to echo-chambers for Marianne's loud sensibilities or an amanuensis for the jealous Miss Grey.

Ultimately, Elinor is relieved that Marianne and Willoughby never married. She recognizes that his selfishness, extravagance, and vanity would have conspired to make both miserable:

> Your marriage must have involved you in many certain troubles and disappointments in which you would have been poorly supported by an affection, on his side, much less certain. Had you married, you must have been always poor. His expensiveness is acknowledged even by himself, and his whole conduct declares that self-denial is a word hardly understood by him. His demands and your inexperience together on a small, very small income, must have brought on distresses which would not be the *less* grievous to you from having been entirely unknown and unthought before. *Your* sense of honour and honesty would have led you, I know, when aware of your situation, to attempt all the economy that would appear to you possible; and perhaps, as long as your frugality retrenched only on your own comfort, you might have been suffered to practise it, but beyond that—and how little could

the utmost of your single management do to stop the ruin which had begun before your marriage?—Beyond *that*, had you endeavoured, however reasonably, to abridge *his* enjoyments is it not to be feared that instead of prevailing on feelings so selfish to consent to it, you would have lessened you own influence on his heart, and made him regret the connection which had involved him in such difficulties. (p. 248)

This is a difficult truth for Marianne to accept. When Elinor first judges Willoughby to be selfish from first to last, Marianne can hardly believe it. She eventually comes round to accept her sister's assessment, and in so doing comes to know more of her own selfishness as well. Though she seems a diminished creature at the end, quietly accepting Brandon's attentions and marrying him, in fact she has come to possess more true sensibility than she ever has.

Willoughby gets off fairly easily considering the dissipation of his character. His selfish sensibility leads at worst to a comfortable and fairly idle life without affection. Through her selfish sense, Lucy Steele is able to achieve even better results. By deftly abandoning Edward when he is disinherited and taking up with his foppish and "puppyish" brother Robert, she is able to gain the wealthy man she had hoped for. This is not what Elinor expected:

Elinor's curiosity to see Mrs. Ferrars was satisfied. She had found in her everything that could tend to make a further connection between the families undesireable. She had seen enough of her pride, her meanness, and her determined prejudice against herself, to comprehend all the difficulties that must have perplexed the engagement, and retarded the marriage of Edward and herself, had he been otherwise free; and she had seen almost enough to be thankful for her own sake, that one greater obstacle preserved her from suffering under any other of Mrs. Ferrars's creation, preserved her from all dependence upon her caprice, or any solicitude for her good opinion. Or at least, if she did not bring herself quite to rejoice in Edward's being fettered to Lucy, she determined, that had Lucy been more amiable, she *ought* to have rejoiced.

She wondered that Lucy's spirits could be so very much elevated by the civility of Mrs. Ferrars; that her interest and her vanity should so very much blind her, as to make the attention which seemed only paid her because she was *not Elinor*, appear a compliment to herself—or to allow her to derive encouragement from a preference only given her, because her real situation was unknown. (p. 168)

Elinor captures Mrs. Ferrars exactly and also recognizes that her favor toward Lucy was out of spite for her. She has exegeted the initial situation accurately. Yet, she is mistaken about the ultimate outcome. She underestimates what a determined devotion to self-interest might bring; like Willoughby, Lucy's story is a parable: "A most encouraging instance of what an earnest, an unceasing attention to self-interest, however its progress may be apparently obstructed, will do in securing every advantage of fortune, with no other sacrifice than that of time and conscience" (p. 267). Austen is a moralist, but, as John Lauber has put it, she is not a "punitive" moralist. Sometimes her villains receive no more serious punishment than to achieve their desires. Often that is punishment enough.

Secrecy and the revelation of secrets plague the relationships and romances of the characters nearly to the end. Mrs. Ferrars disinherits Edward when his secret engagement to Lucy becomes public, and Brandon, seeking to be useful as always, intervenes to offer Edward a living as a clergyman. He asks Elinor to communicate the message, without knowing anything of her long-standing love for Edward. Brandon thus unknowingly asks Elinor to assist in providing Edward with the means for going forward with his plans to marry Lucy; that is, Brandon asks Elinor to take a part in destroying her own hopes for happiness with Edward and in destroying Edward by securing a wife that he does not love. This leads to further, more comic confusions when Mrs. Jennings assumes that Brandon has asked Elinor to marry him.

Even more painful is the unexpected arrival of Edward when Elinor and Lucy are meeting together. To have all the members of the triangle in the same room is awkward enough, but then Marianne arrives, still confident that Elinor and Edward are moving toward engagement and wholly ignorant of Lucy's relationship with Edward. Every word that Marianne speaks is a blunder, and increases the pain and discomfort of everyone else. Edward compliments Marianne on her improved looks, and she replies "don't think of *my* health. Elinor is well, you see. That must be enough for both of us." When she complains that Edward had not visited them, he replies the he was "engaged" elsewhere, drawing this from Marianne: "Engaged! But what was that, when such friends were to be met?" Lucy Steele charges that Marianne believes that "young men never stand upon engagements, if they have no mind to keep them, little as well as great" (pp. 171–172). The issue is not only the pain caused by secret alliances, but also Marianne's continuing insensibility to the realities of what is happening; after Lucy Steele's remark, Elinor observes that "Marianne seemed entirely insensible of the sting."

Happiness comes when all the secrets are revealed, when everything whispered behind closed doors is shouted from the housetops. And it might seem, then, that Austen would join Marianne in attacking the institutions and gestures of manners and marriage that force secrecy and produce so much pain. Austen's point, however, is far more subtle, and, as Tony Tanner suggests, almost Freudian. According to Freud, society consists of structures and institutions that limit and constrain our desires; we cannot do all we desire to do and this causes us pain. Yet, this restraint is the cost we pay for living civilized lives and it is worth the price. The sane and balanced man is one whose "ego" has learned to navigate between desire (the "id") and social expectations (the "superego"). Austen has a keen sense of the ironies and pains that secrecy causes, but recognizes also that this is a necessary part of social life. A world of complete openness and extreme sensibility would be far more painful, and would in fact become "insensible."

Yet Austen's point is in the end more Christian than Freudian. She affirms the necessity of secrecy not because it is inevitable or practical. Elinor is Austen's model not because she stoically endures the anguish of a painful secret. She is a model because, though a lover of Edward, she did not love "only him." She is a model because her acceptance of secrecy makes it possible for her to be sensible, in both senses of that rich word.

Review Questions

1. How are Elinor's and Marianne's romances parallel to each other?

2. How do the two sisters react to their disappointments?

3. Why do their reactions differ so completely? What does this say about Marianne's "sensibility"?

4. How does Austen recover some sympathy for Willoughby? What is Elinor's final assessment of his character?

5. How does Willoughby's character compare to the other men?

6. What "lesson" does Austen draw from Lucy Steele's "success"? Is she serious?

Thought Questions

1. What does Marianne think of Mrs. Jennings? Is this a fair assessment of her? What does it tell us about Marianne?

2. How does Elinor first meet Edward's brother Robert? What kind of man is he?

3. More than once, Elinor believes false rumors about Edward's future marriage. Who relays these rumors to her? How do these reports fit into larger issues of the book?

4. In chapter thirty-four, there is a discussion of the relative heights of Harry Dashwood and William Middleton. How does this discussion reveal the characters?

5. Explain how Fanny Dashwood's meanness to Elinor and Marianne backfires in chapter thirty-six.

CHAPTER 5

"I Cannot Act":
Mansfield Park

In Whit Stillman's intriguing Austenesque film *Metropolitan*, Tom Townsend, the young man from across town who has been befriended by the group of debutantes and preppies, is astonished when Audrey Rouget, the leading female character, reveals that she enjoys *Mansfield Park*. Everyone knows, Tom says, that *Mansfield Park* is the worst novel Jane Austen wrote and nobody likes the book's heroine, Fanny Price. Audrey, the moral center of the film and very much a Fanny Price character herself, protests simply, "*I* like Fanny Price." It is later revealed that Tom has never read *Mansfield Park* or anything else by Jane Austen. He says he prefers to read critics. At Audrey's urging, Tom eventually reads some Austen and is delighted with it.

Tom certainly had his choice of critics to support his hostility to *Mansfield Park* and Fanny Price. To be sure, *Mansfield Park* has not always been as sharply criticized as it is today. During Austen's lifetime, it vied with *Pride and Prejudice* as Austen's best-loved novels. Even today, Tony Tanner perceptively (and, in my judgment, accurately) calls *Mansfield Park* one of the "most profound novels" of the nineteenth century. Yet the novel and its heroine have endured sharp attacks. Lord David Cecil said that Fanny was "a little wooden, a little charmless, and rather a prig." Kingsley Amis was vicious: Fanny is "a monster of complacency and pride." Another saw her as "the most terrible incarnation we have of the female prig-pharisee," and C. S. Lewis found little to admire: Fanny has "nothing except rectitude of mind; neither passion, nor physical courage, nor wit, nor resource." Others have suggested that Fanny makes a fatal mistake in rejecting the vivacious, interesting, and very rich Henry Crawford in favor of the dull and stiff clergyman Edmund Bertram.

And there are characters in the book who share Tom's dislike of Fanny. When Fanny resists Henry's advances, Sir Thomas, her uncle and guardian, lashes into her for ingratitude:

> I had thought you peculiarly free from wilfulness of temper, self-conceit, and every tendency to that independence of spirit, which prevails so much in modern days, even in young women, and which in young women is offensive and disgusting beyond all common offence. But you have now shewn me that you can be wilful and perverse, that you can and will decide for yourself, without any consideration or deference for those who have surely some right to guide you—without even asking their advice. You have shewn yourself very, very different from any thing that I imagined. . . . You do not owe me the duty of a child. But, Fanny, if your heart can acquit you of *ingratitude*. . . . (pp. 318–319)[†]

Spoken in anger and frustration, these words do not represent Sir Thomas's final verdict on Fanny. Much more consistently hostile is Mrs. Norris, Fanny's widowed aunt, who persistently shares the critical belief that Fanny is proud and priggish and ungrateful.

Of course, few critics want to be classed with the bullying Mrs. Norris. But their attacks on Fanny show that they are as incapable of seeing her qualities as Mrs. Norris is, and indeed incapable of following Austen's clear directions for judging Fanny. It is often pointed out that of all of Austen's heroines, Fanny is one of only two (Anne Elliot is the other) who is not treated with irony, who does not make any serious misjudgment, whose behavior is always supported by the narrator. Elizabeth Bennet willfully misjudges Darcy, Emma misjudges everything, Catherine Morland is for most of *Northanger Abbey* too ignorant to form judgments,

---

[†] Page numbers are taken from the Penguin Classics edition (1981), edited by Tony Tanner.

and even the sensible Elinor Dashwood collects enough mistakes to fill a small cupboard. Unless we are to suspect Austen of a hyper-ironic stance where Austen's *lack* of irony toward Fanny is a way of reinforcing irony, then we should accept at face value that Austen considers Fanny morally and intellectually exemplary.

To be sure, Fanny—physically weak, easily fatigued, often painfully shy and backward, with little wit—suffers in many respects by comparison to the other characters of the book. She is indeed an unusual heroine. Mary Crawford is thoroughly her brother's sister, full of wit and life and sparkle, a secular angel who charms Edmund Bertram by playing the harp. Julia and Maria Bertram, Edmund's sisters, are more accomplished than Fanny. Of the male characters, Edmund is surely the least immediately attractive. Not only Henry, but Tom Bertram, Edmund's wastrel older brother and John Yates, the fervent actor, seem more interesting. Rushworth, who marries Maria, is a dolt cut from the same cloth as Mr. Collins in *Pride and Prejudice*, but his very doltishness makes him fun to read about. In such a company, Edmund and Fanny are definitely not the standouts.

Yet given Austen's clear signals that they are the most moral and the central characters in the book, we have to say that this contrast is deliberate and, further, that critics who side with the Crawfords against Edmund and Fanny are falling into the same trap as those Blakean critics who think that Milton was on the devil's side without knowing it. No doubt other characters are more immediately and superficially brilliant—but that is just the point. Austen wants our judgments about her characters to be shaped by the *principles* they display, not by their ability to charm. Charm deceives, and many are the critics who are taken in by it. Fanny's weakness and immobility are also part of the point. She shares much with classic Christian heroines, like Constance in Chaucer's "Man of Law's Tale," who are heroines of *perseverance*. When Fanny refuses to marry Henry, these are precisely the issues in play: She distrusts Henry's character and principles, and her heart is already committed to Edmund. Consistent with this perseverance, Fanny spends much of the novel in a single location, Mansfield Park, while many of the other characters come and go, and in several scenes Fanny sits in the center of a swirl of activity. This is not a fault. Her very *immobility*, her stillness in a world running after vanity, makes her a heroine.

Fanny's patient endurance in the midst of upheaval is connected with her persistent and winning gratitude. She is definitely not the ingrate that Sir Thomas suspects she is; on the contrary, because she does not pursue anything, everything comes to her as sheer gift. And she knows it. She is effusive in her praise of creation in a way that is not characteristic of Austen's heroines. When Marianne praises "dead leaves" in *Sense and Sensibility*, Austen expects us to laugh at her (as the other characters do). But there is no ironic overtone at Fanny's wonder at the beauty of the gardens of Mansfield Park:

> My uncle's gardener always says the soil here is better than his own, and so it appears from the growth of laurels and evergreens in general.—The evergreen!—How beautiful, how welcome, how wonderful the evergreen!—When one thinks of it, how astonishing a variety of nature!—In some countries we know the tree that sheds its leaf is the variety, but that does not make it less amazing, that the same soil and the same sun should nurture plants different in the first rule and law of their existence. You will think me rhapsodizing; but when I am out of doors, especially when I am sitting out of doors, I am very apt to get into this sort of wondering strain. One cannot fix one's eyes on the commonest natural production without finding food for a rambling fancy. (p. 223)

Among other things, this passage helps to establish the contrast between Fanny's character and Mary's, who walks beside her "untouched and inattentive" (p. 222). A city girl, Mary is more concerned about the ins and outs of fashion and etiquette than she is about gardens. For Mary, the world is something to be mastered, manipulated, and made; for Fanny, the world is a gift to be received with thanksgiving. Fanny is the eucharistic heroine, giving thanks in all times and places.

Tony Tanner has made something of the same point, but on a

wider, political and social context. *Mansfield Park* was written near the end of the Napoleonic Wars, during a time of tumultuous change and serious threats to Britain. The threats that Austen identifies in the novel, however, were not the obvious threats to England's stability and peace—French invasions, Jacobin spying, and the like. Rather she sees the threat embodied in a particular way of life, one that detaches moral principle from good breeding and mannerliness. That distinction is made explicit in the book during a conversation among Mary, Fanny, and Edmund in part one. Edmund has insisted that the clergy shapes the manners of a nation, but Mary does not believe it:

> With regard to their influencing public manners, Miss Crawford must misunderstand me, or suppose I mean to call them the arbiters of good breeding, the regulators of refinement and courtesy, the masters of the ceremonies of life. The *manners* I speak of, might rather be called *conduct*, perhaps, the result of good principle. (p. 121)

With regard to "refinement and courtesy," the Crawfords are without equal in the book. But that does not mean they conduct themselves according to good principles, which is the true meaning of "good manners." Fanny's comments on the variety of nature apply here: it is wondrous that the same (English) soil and the same sun should produce "plants differing in the first rule and law of their existence." If England is going to continue breeding truly "good manners," Edmund argues, faithful pastors are essential.

This distinction of good breeding and good principles is developed and broadened in connection with two other main themes. The first of these is acting. A central scene in the book is the home theatrical production that the young people plan during Sir Thomas's absence, over the objections of Edmund (at least initially) and Fanny. (This is one of the main charges against Fanny—she is a prude because she is so resolute in condemning a harmless entertainment.) But the acting theme is pervasive. Henry is a natural actor on stage and a public reader of considerable power.

Even when Fanny is trying to resist his advances, she cannot help but be fascinated by his reading of a passage from Shakespeare. Henry is a wonderful actor because he is *always* acting. Fanny recognizes this from the beginning—he trifles, he flirts, at every moment he is playing a part. That makes him charming, not least to many readers; but we as readers are supposed to be learning to see through his playacting, and search instead, as Fanny does, for strong principles and upright character.

The second related theme is a geographic one. Space almost plays the role of a character in the book. Not only do certain towns have important thematic associations, but the living space has a subtle influence on character. Fanny's life is divided between two locations. Early in the novel, she moves from her family's home in Portsmouth to live with her uncle and aunt Bertram at Mansfield Park. Her large family lived in cramped housing, and Fanny is at first overwhelmed by the size of everything at Mansfield:

> The grandeur of the house astonished, but could not console her. The rooms were too large for her to move in with ease; whatever she touched she expected to injure, and she crept about in constant terror of something or other; often retreating towards her own chamber to cry; and the little girl who was spoken of in the drawing-room when she left at night, as seeming so desirably sensible of her peculiar good fortune, ended every day's sorrows by sobbing herself to sleep. (p. 51)

To make the Park a livable space, Fanny sets up a little "nest of comforts" in the East room, where she retreats to read and think. Even there, the fact that she is marginal to Mansfield Park is emphasized by the fact that Mrs. Norris allows no fire in the room.

Fanny eventually adjusts to the space of Mansfield, and this is most dramatically evident during her return trip to visit her family in Portsmouth in book three:

> Fanny was almost stunned. The smallness of the house, and the thinness of the walls, brought every thing so close to her, that, added to the fatigue of her journey, and all her recent

agitation, she hardly knew how to bear it. *Within* the room all was tranquil enough, for Susan having disappeared with the others, there were soon only her father and herself remaining; and he taking out a newspaper—the accustomary loan of a neighbour, applied himself to studying it, without seeming to recollect her existence. The solitary candle was held between himself and the paper, without any reference to her possible convenience; but she had nothing to do, and was glad to have the light screened from her aching head, as she sat in bewildered, broken, sorrowful contemplation.

She was at home. (p. 375)

Space may be cramped, but she is as distant from everyone as she ever was as a child at Mansfield. The only light is the candle held by her father, and she is screened from it by her father's newspaper. Instead of creating a circle of light in which two might sit, the light illumines only one.

The loneliness of Portsmouth is not the main problem, however. The main problem is a complete lack of order. Chaos is the ruling order of the Price home:

Here, everybody was noisy, every voice was loud, (excepting, perhaps, her mother's, which resembled the soft monotony of Lady Bertram's, only worn into fretfulness.)—Whatever was wanted, was halloo'd for, and the servants halloo'd out their excuses from the kitchen. The doors were constantly banging, the stairs were never at rest, nothing was done without a clatter, nobody sat still, and nobody could command attention when they spoke. (p. 384)

Fanny's story is symbolized by this move from Portsmouth to Mansfield and back. She comes from the chaos and disorderliness of Portsmouth and is formed into a young woman by Mansfield. Mansfield has the classic English virtues of repose, quietness, and stoic endurance. It is a country place in contrast to the bustling port city of Portsmouth. It takes the raw material of a Portsmouth and transforms it into a noble woman. The influence of place on character and even appearance is highlighted by Fanny's contemplation of her mother's looks during their walk to church: "Her poor mother now did not look so very unworthy of being Lady Bertram's sister as she was but too apt to look. It often grieved her to the heart—to think of the contrast between them—to think that where nature had made so little difference, circumstances should have made so much, and that her mother, as handsome as Lady Bertram, and some years her junior, should have an appearance so much more worn and faded, so comfortless, so slatternly, so shabby" (p. 400). That was Fanny's future, but for the intervention of Mansfield Park. To this extent, the novel could be seen as a celebration of the values of the English nobility.

But all is not well at the Park either, and that is so largely because a third location is also thematically significant—London. Henry and Mary Crawford come to Mansfield Park from London and bring London with them. London is the maker of manners, the pacesetter for all things fashionable—or so the Crawfords think. Mary cannot wait to get back to London, but in the meantime, she and her brother help to set up an outpost of London manners at Mansfield. The Crawfords desire for entertainment, their need for amusement, their impatience with old ways and their eagerness always to be attempting some novelty infects the rest of the young people at Mansfield Park. Henry agrees to act because it is among those pleasures he has never had, and he talks persistently about "improvements" at Rushworth's Sotherton and even at Edmund's parish home in Thornton Lacey. London is a city of actors, full of people who, having no settled place in life, are constantly trying on some new role. One dimension of the conflict of the novel lies here: who is to be the maker of manners? London or the church?

Of course, the perversion of the nobility at Mansfield Park is not altogether London's fault. Even before Henry and Mary arrive, it is clear that something is amiss. Good breeding and good conduct have already been separated, as Sir Thomas has singularly failed to pass on his own sense of propriety and morals to his children. Maria and Julia are well-educated "in everything but disposition," and though they mock Fanny for not knowing the "principal rivers in Russia," they are "entirely deficient in the less common acquirements of self-knowledge, generosity and humility," all subjects in which Fanny excels (pp. 54–55). Tom, the eldest Bertram, is even worse, a ne'er-do-well who has none of his father's sense of responsibility for the moral climate of the Bertram house or for the repute of the Bertram name. In part, Austen is focusing attention on the collapsing morals of the upper classes of England. *Mansfield Park*'s cast of characters is socially much higher than the characters in Austen's other novels. Henry and Mary have been exceedingly rich for some years, Rushworth has twelve thousand pounds, and the Bertrams have no monetary wants or cares. Put energetic young people in a house, remove adult restraint, stir in several thousands of pounds: That, Austen thinks, is a recipe for disaster.

One of the results of the detachment of breeding from true manners—symbolized by acting and by the influence of London values on the wealthy inhabitants of the Park—is the development of individualism. We have already noted in the introduction that Austen recognized that a moral life is always lived in community. We need others to guide and teach us, and several of Austen's novels hinge on the ability of a woman to find a suitable mentor (Emma finds Knightley, Catherine Morland finds Henry Tilney). Living in community also means recognizing that our actions are not our own, but always have effects on others. However Aristotelian Austen was in other respects, she implicitly rejects Aristotle's distinction between "practice" (actions whose effects remain with the actor) and "poesis" (actions whose effects go beyond the actor), for she knows that every action is poetic.

Henry and Mary Crawford do not recognize the inherent poetry of life. They are perfect individualists. They are individualists in the sense that they follow their own desires regardless of what authorities say or do. When Sir Thomas is away on business, they take part in a theatrical production and in fact press for it, even though they are warned that the master of the house would disapprove and even over the initial objections of Edmund, who is responsible for managing the house in his father's absence. More subtly but equally importantly, they have no sense that their actions have consequences beyond the individual. When Henry runs away with Maria, now Mrs. Rushworth, Mary Crawford is still hoping that Edmund will want to marry her. She is utterly insensible to the fact that Henry's scandal might affect *her* in any way. Finally, they are individualists because they are *actors*. An actor chooses one role today, and another role tomorrow. His "role" is not defined by anyone or anything around him, but solely by his choice. His purpose in life is not determined by his heritage or his family or his "vocation." It is determined only by himself. A social "actor" is always an "individualist."

I have said in another chapter that because of its emphasis on charity, *Emma* is the most thoroughly Christian novel that Austen wrote. The main rival for that claim is *Mansfield Park*, and in this novel the Christian themes are more overt. Edmund is destined to be a clergyman, much to the astonishment of Mary Crawford, who thinks that clergymen are "nothing." Several of the key conversations in the novel are concerned with the issue of calling, the role of the clergy in the nation, and the contrast between the clergy of London and the clergy in the rest of England. The above quotation from Edmund is part of his defense for the indispensability of the church for the health of the nation, and the illness that the upper classes of the novel are suffering is symbolized by the neglected and vacant chapel at Rushworth's Sotherton. Mary expresses the modern secularist mind set; when told that morning prayers have been discontinued at Sotherton, she smiles and says, "Every generation has its improvements" (p. 115). Improvements again! It is especially in *Mansfield Park* that Austen displays her abilities as a public theologian.

Edmund's calling lends an almost allegorical tone to the story. Edmund, the future guardian of morals, is attracted to the flashy novelty of Mary Crawford of London and fails for some time to see her true character. Choosing this woman would lead him far from his calling and, because the clergy are the protectors of morals, would contribute by omission to the decline of English morals. Eventually, however, he chooses the modest and moral Fanny Price. He is set up to choose between Lady Wisdom and Lady Folly, between the true Church and the false. The book is a comedy because he makes the right choice. If there is a meta-irony in *Mansfield Park*, it is not that Austen secretly mocks Fanny; it is rather that Austen, the ironist, realist, and literalist, is Bunyan's blood-sister.

When Austen talked about the purpose and theme of *Mansfield Park*, she said she was writing on the subject of ordination, with the related themes of vocation or calling. That referred of course to Edmund's calling to be a clergyman and the temptation to abandon that vocation when Mary appears. The challenge before Edmund is to persevere in the role that he has been ordained to fill and to resist the temptation to become an actor-individualist. And this is the same temptation that confronts Fanny: she has been "ordained" to love Edmund, and she must persevere through persistent temptations from Henry Crawford. Austen brings the two "vocations" of marriage and ordination into direct connection. While everyone is expectantly awaiting the Mansfield ball, Edmund has his mind on other things, being "deeply occupied in the consideration of the two important events now at hand, which were to fix his fate in life—ordination and matrimony" (p. 262). If there is allegory here, it cuts both ways: not only must the shepherd resist the allurements of the false woman, but the bride must resist the advances of a charming but ultimately scurrilous suitor. Both must be faithful to their "fixed fates."

Vocation is set in direct contrast to acting. Both have to do with taking on and playing "roles," but the meaning of "role" in the two cases is quite different. An actor might adopt many different roles, none of which defines who he is. Actors have no "fixed fate" in life. Thus, in contrast to the "actors" of the story, Edmund is "called" to a particular "vocation." Even though, as he emphasizes to Mary, he has chosen to pursue the ministry, in a more profound sense he has *been chosen*. And his role is not determined by the whims of the moment but by assuming a particular position within English society, a position established by the ritual of ordination, which determines the role he is going to play. He is not free to choose another "role" tomorrow. For a called man or woman, his or her role is not a mask that can be removed at will. The mask sticks so closely to his face as to be permanent. The health of Mansfield, and of England, depends on which path is chosen—on whether the next generation chooses to be "actors" or accepts "ordination."

Review Questions

1. What is the common critical view of Fanny Price? Why?

2. What is Austen trying to say by making Fanny a heroine?

3. How does the story of *Mansfield Park* reflect some of the large political events of Austen's day?

4. Discuss the different views of "manners" that are evident among the characters of the book.

5. How does the geographic theme work out in the book?

6. How are Henry and Mary Crawford "individualists"?

7. How does Edmund's calling to be a pastor fit into the themes of the book? Discuss the contrast between calling and acting.

Book One

Fanny Price is brought from Portsmouth to Mansfield Park as a ten-year-old girl, and she is overwhelmed by the place and the people. The people incarnate the place. Sir Thomas, her uncle, is a principled man, not at all like the dissolute young baronets who take over his house in his absence. He is kind toward his inert wife and takes steps to ensure that she is always cared for. Later he discerns Maria's dissatisfaction with Rushworth and offers to deliver her from a bad match. Though he has admirable qualities and acts uprightly, he loves his position too much, shows too little love and care for Fanny, and therefore is a terror to her. Maria and Julia have been instructed not to treat Fanny as an equal, something they hardly needed reminding about.

Mrs. Norris, Fanny's aunt, has no redeeming qualities. She has a "love of money" that is "equal to her love of direction, and she knew quite as well how to save her own as to spend that of her friends" (p. 45). She is domineering and bullying toward Fanny. She constantly reminds Fanny that she is out of place at Mansfield and consistently belittles her and accuses her of ingratitude. She blames Fanny for everything; when Maria later runs away with Henry, she complains that it would never have happened if only Fanny had accepted Henry's offer of marriage. She complains that she is always the one to take things in hand, when in fact she is always the last one to raise a finger to assist another. Fanny begins to make progress and to settle in more comfortably when she is "no longer materially afraid to appear before her uncle" and when "her aunt Norris's voice [ceased to] make her start very much" (p. 53).

Among the members of the house, only Edmund shows Fanny any genuine kindness. When she wishes to write her brother William, he provides pen and paper. That encounter seals Fanny's affection, not only for its basic kindliness but also because it is a favor to her brother, whom she adores. This foreshadows Henry's much greater favor toward William later in the book, but that favor is actually quite different from Edmund's. Edmund acts out of genuine sympathy for his lonely cousin, while Henry helps William only to have another card to play in his pursuit of Fanny.

Two large themes are introduced in the characterizations that are provided in the opening chapters. First, the issue of idleness and work, of rest and restlessness, are raised in connection with the members of the Bertram family. As always in Austen, there is a spectrum rather than a simple opposition. At one end, there is the virtually immobile Lady Bertram, who is constantly being served though she is in herself a sweet and undemanding nullity:

> To the education of her daughters, Lady Bertram paid not the smallest attention. She had not time for such cares. She was a woman who spent her days in sitting nicely dressed on a sofa, doing some long piece of needlework, of little use and no beauty, thinking more of her pug than her children, but very indulgent to the latter, when it did not put herself to inconvenience, guided

in every thing important by Sir Thomas, and in smaller concerns by her sister. (p. 55)

Austen is not harsh with Lady Bertram, but she certainly does not present her as an ideal. Her idleness is an extreme version of that noble detachment that the younger characters will misuse in the play scenes.

At the other end of the spectrum is aunt Norris, always a bustle of activity. She is not an actor, but prefers "directing." But this too is a flaw in Austen's view, and Austen leaves us with much less sympathy for Norris than for Lady Bertram. If idleness is danger-ous, overbearing activity is also. Fanny displays some of the vir-tues of both; though immobile in comparison with some of the other characters, she is consistently useful, especially to Lady Bertram. Throughout the novel Fanny, having received comfort from Edmund, is a source of comfort for her aunt Bertram.

The issue of activity *versus* idleness is taken up in the frequent discussion of "improvements." The question first comes up dur-ing a conversation between Henry and Rushworth. Rushworth has little idea what he wants to improve, or why or how: "I have no eye or ingenuity for such matters," he rightly says (p. 88). Since he has no ability, he plans to hire an expert in improve-ments to visit Sotherton and improve it. This is a perfect symbol of the modern spirit—an itch for novelty, allied with a depen-dence on experts. These discussions symbolize the lust for novelty that Austen identifies as personal motivation for the Crawfords: "It doesn't matter what we come up with; so long as it is new, and so long as the experts in new things have a hand in it, then let us move ahead." Rushworth is not much of an actor but his unde-fined desire for "improvement" shows that he is one with the Crawfords. He differs from them mainly in the fact that they are clever and he is very stupid.

A second theme in the opening chapters is sibling relations, which structures much of the story. The book begins with a de-scription of the background of the Ward sisters, who by marriage become Lady Bertram, Aunt Norris, and Mrs. Price. Initially the

story is one of estrangement, and it is not the last story of estranged siblings in the novel. The Bertram family is particularly
fractured: Tom and Edmund Bertram are men of very different
character and there is friction between them, while Julia and Maria
Bertram are rivals for Henry Crawford's affections. On the other
hand, the relations between siblings of different sexes are smooth
and affectionate. Henry and Mary Crawford are unprincipled,
but Fanny recognizes that Mary has a genuine love for her brother.
She is able to recognize that because her love for William is strong.
The most touching "sibling" relation is between the *cousins*,
Edmund and Fanny. Mrs. Norris believes that the fact that they
are brought up as brother and sister would make any romance
between them "morally impossible" (p. 44). This shows how little
Norris knows about romance, at least romance Austen style. For
many of Austen's characters, romance is born out of something
very like a sibling relationship. Edmund and Fanny as "siblings"
are early on set up in contrast to the sibling "actors," Henry and
Mary Crawford.

One of the recurring scenes in the novel involves a pair of "siblings" in conversation concerning events at the Park. Apart from
their early childhood conversation, Fanny and Edmund are seen
in serious and extended conversations in at least five chapters (7,
12, 21, 35, 47). Lengthy conversations between Henry and Mary
Crawford take up large portions of three chapters (5, 24, 29), and
in each case is an important commentary on the story. One of the
striking differences between these sets of conversations is that Henry
and Mary are normally plotting and conspiring to achieve something in the future, while Fanny and Edmund are seeking to understand what is happening in the present. Henry and Mary are
devoted to "improvements" and pushing things in new directions;
for Fanny and Edmund, the world is much more a *given*, something they have to respond to rightly rather than force into the
shape of their desires.

London comes to Mansfield in the form of Henry and Mary
Crawford. Henry is thought plain by everyone, until his
charming and flirtatious ways, as well as his large income, begin

to inflame Maria's and Julia's imaginations. Only Fanny remains convinced that he is quite plain. Mary is pretty and lively and shows an immediate interest in Tom Bertram, though she shortly shifts attention to his brother Edmund. Henry's manners are so good that Mrs. Grant, his sister, imputes to him all other good qualities (p. 74), and though initially finding him "plain and black," the Bertram sisters are so taken by his manners that they decide that he is exceedingly good-looking (p. 78). "Manners" here should be taken in the sense of flirtatious attentions, which Henry bestows in great measure.

As a role-playing actor, Henry's behavior does not flow from or produce order and decorum; on the contrary, his conduct leads to continuous upheaval and chaos. Though elegant, rich, and well-mannered, he is a Satan who delights in the chaos that he causes. It is not merely that he has no "fixed fate" and no "calling"; he refuses to recognize the "fixed fate" of others and attempts to seduce them from their vocations. During one of his early conversations with his sister, he says that he prefers the engaged Maria Bertram to her younger sister Julia:

> An engaged woman is always more agreeable than a disengaged. She is satisfied with herself. Her cares are over, and she feels that she may exert all her powers of pleasing without suspicion. All is safe with a lady engaged; no harm can be done. (p. 78)

This turns the purpose of an engagement upside down. The purpose is not to free the engaged woman to flirt without suspicion but to limit her relations with other men. Henry would turn engagement into disengagement.

Henry's delight in chaos is even more explicit later, when he reflects on the fun the young people all had planning the play:

> I shall always look back on our theatricals with exquisite pleasure. There was such an interest, such an animation, such a spirit diffused! Every body felt it. We were all alive. There was employment, hope, solicitude, bustle, for every hour of the day. Always

some little objection, some little doubt, some little anxiety to be got over. I never was happier. (p. 236)

Fanny silently condemns him: "never happier than when behaving so dishonourably and unfeelingly!— Oh! what a corrupted mind!" (p. 236).

Mary Crawford is the female version of her brother, an actress and opportunist. Her character is established in part by contrast with Fanny. One particularly striking example is found in book two (chapter twenty-two), during the same conversation where Fanny rhapsodizes on the beauties of evergreens. Fanny is commenting on the wonderful changes that have taken place in the grounds at Mansfield Park and this leads her into an astonished meditation on memory:

> How wonderful, how very wonderful the operations of time, and the changes of the human mind! . . . If any one faculty of our nature may be called *more* wonderful than the rest, I do think it is memory. There seems something more speakingly incomprehensible in the powers, the failures, the inequalities of memory, than in any other of our intelligences. The memory is sometimes so retentive, so serviceable, so obedient—at others, so bewildered and so weak—and at other again, so tyrannic, so beyond control!—we are to be sure a miracle every way—but our powers of recollecting and of forgetting, do seem peculiarly past finding out. (p. 222)

This is a striking statement in many ways: it is a celebration of memory worthy of Augustine, whose *Confessions* remain the classic on the subject. The "past finding out" is clearly a biblical or liturgical reference that indicates that Fanny is attributing the mystery of memory to God. But the most striking thing about this statement is Mary's reaction: "Miss Crawford, untouched and inattentive, had nothing to say" (p. 222) and is most astonished to see herself in such a place. Not only does Mary have no sense of the beauty of the creation or the wonders of the human mind, she simply has no memory—she is all new. This is of a piece with her individualism and acting: an actor needs no memory of a past, since he can always adopt a new past at will; an individualist wants no past, since having a past would limit his choices in the present.

Structurally, book one (chapters 1–18) may be diagramed as follows:

chap. 1–3	chap. 4–18: Sir Thomas's absence			
Introduction	4–5	6–10	11–12	13–18
	gathering	Sotherton	gathering	theater

With this diagram I am seeking to highlight several features of book one. First, one of the defining aspects of the situation in chapters 4–18 is that Sir Thomas is absent. In his absence Mansfield is left in the hands of a younger cast of characters, supposedly under the guidance of Lady Bertram and Aunt Norris. Instead of controlling things, these merely let the young people have their way, with results that are a minor catastrophe that eventually lead to a major one. Sir Thomas's control of the house is established as soon as he returns home at the beginning of book two: He brings an immediate end to the theatrical production, and then he quickly takes steps to undo the damage done by the day at Sotherton (during which, as we shall see, Henry Crawford and Maria Bertram conduct themselves badly).

Second, the structure described above highlights the connections between the day that the young people spend at Sotherton and the time they spend preparing for the theatrical production at Mansfield. This connection is important for understanding Fanny's (and Austen's) evaluation of the theatrical production. Austen was not opposed to theater as such and often produced plays with her siblings in her own home. Her opposition to this particular production arises rather from a recognition of its inner connection with the inappropriate conduct of the characters at Sotherton.

More detailed examination of the two large scenes—the trip to Sotherton and the theatrical production—will show how Austen's themes are developing here. By the time the Rushworths invite the party of young people over to Sotherton, Henry Crawford has already begun to flirt noticeably with Maria, who is already en-gaged to Mr. Rushworth. The day at Sotherton advances that romance several stages. At this point, Julia still has designs on Henry herself and the small group is torn by the rivalries between sisters. Though this conflict causes tensions throughout the day, only Fanny notices. And she notices because only Fanny takes the time to *sit*. Everyone else is on the move, and the whole scene circulates around her; it is a Fanny-centric day.

The circumstances of the tour of the grounds are important, and Austen invests the layout of the grounds with symbolic im-port. For one thing, as Maria says, the town church is well situ-ated at a distance from the house: "The church spire is reckoned remarkably handsome. I am glad the church is not so close to the Great House as often happens in old places. The annoyance of the bells must be terrible" (p. 111). The church is acknowledged only for its contribution to the aesthetics of the town; so long as it does not intrude too closely on the life of the Great House, all is well. Every generation has its improvements, as Mary might say. Simi-larly, the chapel is remarkable for being "fitted up as you see it, in James the Second's time," and because at one time "the linings and cushions of the pulpit and family-seat were only purple cloth." In short, "It is a handsome chapel" (p. 115). Prayers? Oh, they were discontinued in the last generation. But the important thing is that "it is a handsome chapel."

It is in this chapel that the first conversation about clerical office begins. Fanny believes that a family at regular prayer is part of "what such a household should be," but Mary disagrees: "It is safer to leave people to their own devices on such subjects" (p. 115). Even in politics Mary is an individualist, defending lib-erty of conscience in religious matters. She is shocked, then, to learn that Edmund intends to be ordained, and even more shocked that he should have *chosen* the church as a profession: "A clergy-man is nothing," she says, referring to his social standing (p. 120). Edmund gives a spirited defense of the essential place of the clergy in the nation:

A clergyman cannot be high in state or fashion. He must not head mobs, or set the ton in dress. But I cannot call that situation nothing, which has the charge of all that is of the first importance to mankind, individually or collectively considered, temporally and eternally—which has the guardianship of religion and morals, and consequently the manners which result from their influence. No one here can call the *office* nothing. If the man who holds it is so, it is by the neglect of his duty, by foregoing its just importance, and stepping out of his place to appear what he ought not to appear. (p. 120)

Mary cannot believe that the clergy have such weight, since one sees them "so rarely out of his pulpit." But here the contrast of London and the rest of England comes into play; Edmund insists that a proper clergyman is not merely a pulpiteer:

A fine preacher is followed and admired; but it is not in fine preaching only that a good clergyman will be useful in his parish and his neighbourhood, where the parish and neighbourhood are of a size capable of knowing his private character, and observing his general conduct, which in London can rarely be the case. (p. 121)

Several things are happening in this conversation. Clearly, Austen's sympathies are with Edmund, who speaks in tones not unlike his great namesake, Edmund Burke. Edmund's choice is for a high calling, one that does indeed direct the manners and conduct of the nation. Sotherton is "improving," and closing the chapel is one of these improvements. But a house so improved is destined to fall, and Sotherton will fall resoundingly before the end of the novel. Also, Mary's worldliness, her sense of being on the cutting edge of societal evolution, is undercut here with sharp irony. She believes that by knowing London she knows the world: "The metropolis, I imagine, is a pretty fair sample of the rest," and that means if a clergyman is nothing in London he is nothing anywhere (p. 120). On the contrary, Edmund argues, London is a very small and very special world; knowing London does not give Mary knowledge of the world. It is provincial and parochial.

Especially here, the thematic conflict of the novel takes central stage: London *versus* the church.

The geography of the walk at Sotherton is important. The immediate grounds of the house are bounded by a wall and a gate, and then the "wilderness," a wooded and wilder area. During this walk in the "wilderness," Miss Crawford attempts to dissuade Edmund about his clerical calling. It is a kind of temptation scene, in a garden-wilderness, with Mary herself as the forbidden fruit. Austen adds another touch to indicate just how dangerous a position Edmund is in: The entire conversation takes place off the "great path" in the "serpentine" path of the wilderness walk (p. 122). Edmund is tempted to give up his clerical "role" for another; he is tempted to become an actor and leave the great path that is fated for him.

Other temptations follow. Recognizing that Fanny is tired, Edmund sits her down next to a locked gate and walks on with Mary. While Fanny waits, Rushworth walks up with Maria and Henry. They find that the gate is locked and Rushworth returns to the house to fetch a key. Instead of waiting for his return, Maria and Henry go through the gate and walk on. Shortly, Julia comes up; she has been trying to catch up with Maria and Henry, and she too climbs through the gate. Rushworth returns with the key, but it is too late. His party has left him. This farcical scene, which is made all the funnier by the fact that Fanny sits as a spectator through the whole, clearly foreshadows the coming disasters of Sotherton. Maria and Henry will ignore the restrictions of law and morality and run off together; they will crash the gate and make their way into the wilderness. Rushworth, the husband who should be the guardian, will be left standing, holding the key.

The other major scene in book one is the theater scene, which we have already discussed to some extent. Several further comments might be made, however. Given the situation, especially following the trip to Sotherton, Fanny's objections are sound. First, she discerns rightly that Sir Thomas would disapprove of the plans, and she believes, rightly again, that it is wrong to use a man's property in ways he would disapprove. No doubt this is partly due to her consciousness that she has no real rights in the house.

Second, she is the only one who has discerned the inappropriate behavior of Henry and Maria. Her opposition to the theater depends on the knowledge that she received by observing their behavior at Sotherton. Fanny realizes that a play will allow two people an intimacy that is wholly inappropriate. She knows too that the roles that are being assigned and chosen are being chosen precisely so that things can be said that propriety would prohibit in normal conversation. It would not be right for Mary Crawford to declare her love for Edmund in reality; but playing a part in a play will enable her to say things she cannot say in reality. It would not be right for Henry and Maria to go off alone and exchange words of love; but rehearsing the scene from the play gives them leave to do precisely that. More generally, acting is always an opportunity to act in ways that normal social conventions do not permit. A play will permit the lovers to "act" without restraint.

Aside from all this, the symbolic resonances of "acting" have already been established. Edmund is called, approaching ordination; he has a role and need not be searching out another to play. He should say, along with Fanny, "I cannot act."

Review Questions

1. How is Fanny received at Mansfield Park? What does this say about the character of the various Bertrams?

2. Explain the theme of mobility and immobility in establishing characters.

3. What kind of man is Henry Crawford? His sister?

4. How is book one structured? What is the significance of that structure?

5. Explain the significance of the conversation in the chapel at Sotherton.

6. Explain the significance of Henry and Maria going through the gate at Sotherton.

7. Why does Fanny object to the theatrical production at Mansfield?

8. Discuss the symbolism of acting, and of Fanny's refusal to act, in the final chapters of book one.

Thought Questions

1. Who are the Grants? What kind of people are they? How do they fit into the larger themes of the novel?

2. What is the point of the discussion of whether Fanny is "in" or "out"? What does it reveal about Mary Crawford's character?

3. Who does not go to Sotherton? Why is this important?

4. Mary Crawford says that she imagines Sir Thomas as a great hero coming home to sacrifice his children. What kind of sacrifice is she referring to? How does the theme of sacrifice work itself out in the novel?

5. What is the function of the scene of Fanny and Edmund at the window looking at the stars?

Books Two–Three

Part one ends with Edmund and the rest of the players putting pressure on Fanny to participate in the play (p. 191). She has finally agreed to read the part—one of the many indications in the book that Fanny, despite her strong principles, is a perfectly human character. Book three begins with pressure again being put on Fanny, this time pressure for her to accept Henry Crawford's proposal of marriage. Between the two, Henry Crawford has embarked on a new pet project, something to amuse him during his time at Mansfield Park, another "role" to put on. Following Fanny's attendance at dinner at the Grants, Henry announces his plan to his sister:

> "My plan is to make Fanny Price in love with me."
> "Fanny Price! Nonsense! No, no. You ought to be satisfied with her two cousins."

"But I cannot be satisfied without Fanny Price, without making a small hole in Fanny Price's heart." (p. 239)

There is a comic bravado here but overall the effect is horrifying: Here are two wealthy, idle, beautiful people plotting together to "make a small hole" in another person's heart. As egotists and individualists the Crawfords believe other people exist only as means for their amusement. Henry the actor does not just hurt others inadvertently; "murderer" is one of the roles he can play. What he does *not* know is that Fanny's heart is already steeled against his attack because of her love for Edmund. She has already a "fixed fate" and, if she perseveres in her calling, she will be saved from Henry and, allegorically, England will be saved from London's influence.

Brother and sister enter into a conspiracy here, and this conversation and the related conspiratorial conversation in chapter thirty give structure to book two. Between those two conversations, something happens to Henry. Note how different the second conversation is:

> When his sister, who had been waiting for him to walk with her in the garden, met him at last most impatiently in the sweep, and cried out, "My dear Henry, where can you possibly have been all this time?" he had only to say that he had been sitting with Bertram and Fanny.
> "Sitting with them an hour and half!" exclaimed Mary.
> But this was only the beginning of her surprize.
> "Yes, Mary," said he, drawing her arm within his, and walking along the sweep as if not knowing where he was—"I could not get away sooner—Fanny looked so lovely!—I am quite determined, Mary. My mind is entirely made up. Will it astonish you? No—you must be aware that I am quite determined to marry Fanny Price." (p. 295)

Instead of simply acting a part in order to bore a small hole in Fanny's heart, he begins to speak of marriage for the first time. Choosing marriage means having a "fixed fate," and a choice for a fixed fate is the most radical possible change for an actor like Henry. For the first time, he shows himself willing to "sit," to stay in one place and to wear one face. The irony runs in various directions: Henry, not Fanny, is the one whose heart is wounded, and Henry, who aspires to "direct" others for his own purposes, loses control of the situation.

A large part of the drama of book two is the growth of Henry between these two speeches, and a large part of the drama of book three revolves around the question of whether Henry has in fact changed. The verdict on the latter question is ultimately negative; in the end he chooses to disrupt someone else's "fixed fate" rather than to accept one for himself. Even before the final scandal, however, there are signs that Henry has not progressed as far as he appears. Despite his careful attention to Fanny's every gesture and whispered word, despite his willingness to accept her rebukes, he is still and ever Henry—which is to say, he is everybody and nobody.

Several episodes stand out. First, several conversations about the role of clergy indicate that Henry has not really grasped the meaning of "vocation." One conversation in chapter twenty-five significantly takes place during a game of "speculation." Sir Thomas first begins to discern Henry's attention to Fanny and speculates about their future relationship. Fanny speculates about life at Mansfield after Edmund has left to take up his pastoral charge at Thornton Lacey. Henry indulges in speculations of his own, mainly about the "improvements" that could be made to Edmund's future home. Edmund will be satisfied to give the home "the air of a gentleman's residence" but Henry is not content with such minimal improvements:

> You may raise it into a *place*. From being the mere gentleman's residence, it becomes, by judicious improvement, the residence of a man of education, taste, modern manners, good connections. All this may be stamped on it; and that house receive such an air as to make its own be set down as a great land-holder of the parish, by every creature travelling the road. (p. 252)

Henry is still insisting on "improvements" that would make Edmund's pastoral home, like the chapel at Sotherton, into something other than it is. More than that, Henry is still conspiring together with his sister, in this case not to snare Fanny but to snare Edmund. While Henry speaks, Mary has been speculating about going *with* Edmund to his new home but is shocked when she is "no longer able, in the picture she had been forming of a future Thornton, to shut out the church, sink the clergyman, and see only the respectable, elegant, modernized, and occasional residence of a man of independent fortune" (p. 256). Henry and Mary are interested in the parish home at Thornton only so long as they can remove the parish. Every generation has its improvements.

Even after he has declared his intention to settle down and marry Fanny, Henry does not grasp the significance of that decision. This point is again made in a conversation dealing with Edmund's calling. After Henry has read a passage from Shakespeare to good effect, he and Edmund discuss the importance of clerical reading. Edmund agrees that "distinctness and energy" in reading "may have weight in recommending the most solid truths." But Henry's treatment of the subject reduces liturgical reading and preaching to another form of acting:

> A sermon, well delivered, is more uncommon even than prayers well read. A sermon, good in itself, is no rare thing. It is more difficult to speak well than to compose well; that is, the rules and tricks of composition are oftener an object of study. A thoroughly good sermon, thoroughly well delivered, is a capital gratification. I can never hear such a one without the greatest admiration and respect, and more than half a mind to take orders and preach myself. There is something in the eloquence of the pulpit, when it is really eloquence, which is entitled to the highest praise and honour. (p. 338)

Sermonizing is another "role" that Henry would dearly love to play (since it would be new), so long as he could preach only to educated congregations. And not too often: Preaching occasionally would suit, but "not for a constancy; it would not do for a

constancy" (p. 339). But constancy, perseverance, a long obedi-
ence in one direction—this, of course, is precisely the difference
between acting a role and accepting a role as a vocation. When
Henry realizes that Fanny has noted his objection to "constancy,"
Fanny replies: "I thought it a pity you did not always know yourself as well as you seemed to do at that moment."

That Henry's change is superficial is evident not only from the
fact that he misunderstands the nature of calling, but also from
the fact that he consistently attempts to win Fanny's affection
through third parties. This is most strikingly evident in the incident involving the chain. William has given a cross to Fanny,
which she wants to wear over her heart as a sign of her devotion to
her brother. The fact that it is a cross is significant of her Christian virtue, of sacrifice, and particularly the sacrifice associated
with vocation. She is a suffering heroine in many respects, waiting her time out until her lover will see her. The problem was that
she had no chain to put through the cross. Mary offers her one
that she says her brother had given to her, while Edmund gives
Fanny a more delicate chain. She prefers Edmund's but feels obliged
to Henry because he has helped secure a naval promotion for
William, and she ends up wearing both. After the ball, however,
she learns that Henry had given the chain to Mary *in order to* pass
it on to Fanny. Mary serves as the intermediary through whom
Henry is trying to court Fanny. Mary later writes a letter to the
same purpose and makes an open display of her affection. In a
real sense, Fanny is being seduced by *both* brother and sister. The
hint of perversion is brought out much more fully in the film
version of *Mansfield Park* but it is present in the book.

Henry is able to manipulate others to take up his cause as well.
As with the theatrical endeavor, many people join to put pressure
on Fanny, only this time the pressure comes from people she admires: Edmund and Sir Thomas in particular. She is horrified at
Sir Thomas's claim that she is ungrateful and is even more uncomfortable at Edmund's attempts to persuade her to accept his
"friend." When they are not pressuring her to accept Henry,
Edmund and Sir Thomas are leaving her unprotected against
Henry's advances and Aunt Norris's savage attacks.

Fanny's return to Portsmouth is part of the larger conspiracy, a last-ditch effort to make Fanny see reason. Sir Thomas's

> prime motive in sending her away had very little to do with the propriety of her seeing her parents again, and nothing at all with the idea of making her happy. He certainly wished her to go willingly, but he as certainly wished her to be heartily sick of home before her visit ended; and that a little abstinence from the elegancies and luxuries of Mansfield Park, would bring her mind into a sober state, and incline her to a juster estimate of the value of that home of greater permanent, and equal comfort, of which she had the offer. (p. 363)

It nearly works. Henry shows up unexpectedly in Portsmouth, is amiable with Mr. Price, and shows diligent attention to Fanny. Fanny's opposition begins to waver:

> she thought him altogether improved since she had seen him; he was much more gentle, obliging, and attentive to other people's feelings than he had ever been at Mansfield; she had never seen him so agreeable—so *near* being agreeable; his behaviour to her father could not offend, and there was something particularly kind and proper in the notice he took of Susan. He was decidedly improved. (p. 398)

By this time in the novel, however, we should be suspicious of that key term "improved," for Henry has thought of nothing but improvements for most of the book. The improvements he has advocated have all been of the most superficial kind.

Still, the temptation is a real one and Fanny wavers. What keeps her from falling is her sense of vocation, her recognition that she has been called to play a particular role, and her perseverance in that role. The remarkable character of her love for Edmund is highlighted by contrast with the other women characters, who are as catty as they come. Maria, angry at Henry for leaving Mansfield, marries Rushworth out of spite, and Mary is spiteful toward Edmund when he leaves for his ordination. Though Edmund consistently underestimates Fanny and pursues a far inferior woman, Fanny does not turn from her love. Beyond this, however, Edmund recognizes something else at work. When Henry has been exposed as an adulterer, he is worried that Fanny will be deeply hurt. When she assures him that she never loved Henry, he marvels:

> "Thank God!" said he. "We were all disposed to wonder—but it seems to have been the merciful appointment of Providence that the heart which knew no guile, should not suffer. (p. 442)

The faithful heart, loyal to its calling, is spared.

The denouement of the book comes through a series of letters, which completely unveil the Crawfords for the unthinking individualists they are. When Tom Bertram becomes seriously ill, Mary writes to express the hope that the Bertram fortune will now fall into Edmund's more deserving possession. She is willing to accept a clergyman husband, so long as he is sufficiently wealthy and potentially stylish. Even when Henry runs away with Maria Rushworth, Mary thinks that there is no barrier to her continuing connection with Edmund. Mary describes Henry and Maria as "foolish," and the mildness of that judgment offends Edmund: "no harsher name than folly given!—So voluntarily, so freely, so coolly to canvass it!—no reluctance, no horror, no feminine—shall I say? no modest loathings!—This is what the world does" (p. 441). Newly ordained pastor that he is, Edmund is surely using "world" in its fullest biblical sense; worldliness leads only to disaster.

Sir Thomas recognizes too that "this is what the world does." He recognizes the failures of his parenting of his daughters:

> Something had been wanting *within*, or time would have worn away much of its ill effect. He feared that principle, active principle, had been wanting, that they had never been properly taught to govern their inclinations and tempers, by that sense of duty which can alone suffice. They had been instructed theoretically in their religion, but never required to bring it into daily practice. (p. 448)

Like the Rushworth family, Sir Thomas had, symbolically if not in fact, discontinued the prayers that make a house and left the chapel disused and empty. Without a guardian, without a pastor or guide, his daughters had fallen in with "how the world goes."

Edmund is melancholy for only a short time, and then begins to recognize the qualities of his sister-cousin, and that she is precisely the kind of woman he needs at Thornton Lacey. Nearly seduced by the world, nearly led astray by the world to abandon his vocation and become a mere actor, Edmund in the end accepts his calling. "I cannot act," Fanny says. And indeed she cannot, and neither can Edmund. In the end, they both accept, gratefully, their ordained roles, their "fixed fate."

Review Questions

1. How is the end of book one similar to the end of book two?

2. What is Henry Crawford's new plan? How does this turn out? What is ironic about its outcome?

3. Explain how the scenes of Mary and Henry help to structure book two.

4. How does Henry attempt to court Fanny? Explain how this is consistent with his character.

5. How does Fanny resist Henry's temptation?

6. How does Edmund finally resist Mary's temptation?

Thought Questions

1. What do Fanny and Mary talk about when Fanny visits the parsonage? What does this reveal about Mary?

2. How does Henry react when Fanny rebukes him for the play? How does Austen show that this is not entirely sincere?

3. Why does Fanny not reveal to Sir Thomas her reasons for rejecting Henry?

4. In chapter thirty-six, Mary talks about Edmund's decision to participate in acting. How does she describe that? What does this show about her character?

CHAPTER 6

Charity and the "Deeper Game": *Emma*

Pride and Prejudice begins with two young, handsome, wealthy men moving into the neighborhood, intent (or so Mrs. Bennet believes) on finding pretty wives. New faces in Hertfordshire mean new possibilities of change in the social landscape, and these hopes are realized in the course of the novel, as both Jane and Elizabeth Bennet marry above the status of their immediate family and move into more sumptuous dwellings. Lydia Bennet marries Wickham, who comes from outside, and Charlotte moves away to marry Collins. There are no local marriages, and in the end everyone has scattered.

In *Emma*, by contrast, few new faces are to be seen in Highbury, and virtually no one marries outside his station or even outside his home town. The vicar, Mr. Elton, travels to Bath to find a fashionable wife, but then he is not from Highbury himself. Frank Churchill and Jane Fairfax both come from outside the town and they end up married to each other. But all the locals marry locals. Emma marries Mr. Knightley, who has known her from childhood; Miss Taylor, Emma's governess, becomes Mrs. Weston, wife to a well-liked native; Harriet Smith, Emma's protégé, marries Robert Martin, a local farmer. The other main characters—particularly the Bateses—are likewise lifelong residents. By the end of the novel, the Woodhouses are linked by two marriages: Knightley is married to Emma, and his brother John to Emma's sister, Isabella. Nor are there any cross-class marriages in *Emma*:

Elton marries a rich woman, but within his class; Harriet ends up, as she should, with Robert Martin; Emma marries the only man in her life that is of her class. Class structure stays completely in place. It is threatened in various ways in the course of the novel, but is reinforced with a vengeance at the end.

Even physical mobility is limited, particularly for Emma. Emma has lived in Highbury all her life but has never made the seven-mile trip to Box Hill before. Even at the end of the story, when she has married, she and Knightley agree to remain at Hartfield, Emma's home. As one critic has put it, the social world of Highbury is "claustrophobic."

Perhaps the most Christian novel Austen wrote, *Emma* is concerned with the relation of charity and truth; it is about "speaking the truth in love," or more precisely, about truth-speaking as the *path* to love. This is at the heart of the romantic plot of Emma and Mr. Knightley. Everyone else around Emma flatters her, admires her, and generally regards her as a perfect specimen of womanhood. Only Mr. Knightley sees her as the flawed young woman she really is, and only he tells her so, often in very blunt terms. Mr. Knightley is the right man for Emma precisely because he speaks truth.

By placing the romance of Knightley and Emma in the context of this closely knit and unchanging community, Austen raises questions about truth and charity in social life. One evening is described as "everything was relapsing into its usual state. Former provocations reappeared. The aunt was as tiresome as ever." Tanner points out that "as ever" is a perfect description of Highbury, and in a town whose chief characteristic is sameness, old provocations will constantly reappear—unless they are dealt with by truth and love.

The reference to "former provocations" deserves further comment. Though apparently closely knit, Highbury has its share of division and strife; rather, *because* Highbury is close-knit, it has its share of strife. Americans of our century may be naively nostalgic for small-town life, but Austen was not. She knew all about the pettiness, the gossip, the boredom, and the inanity of life in a small community. The most dramatic example of this in *Emma* occurs after Emma's attempt to match Mr. Elton with Harriet ends in disastrous confusion. The painfulness and embarrassment of the situation is made worse by the fact that none of the characters can avoid seeing each other: "Their being so fixed, so absolutely fixed, in the same place, was bad for each, for all three. Not one of them had the power of removal, or of affecting any material change of society. They must encounter each other, and make the best of it." As we shall see below, the Box Hill incident exposes these divisions even more dramatically. G. K. Chesterton once commented on the importance of the fact that God commanded us to love our *neighbors*. We can choose our friends, and they are easy to love because we have chosen them. Our neighbors, however, are simply *given*, simply *there*, and that challenges our love. The residents of Highbury are neighbors, unavoidable to one another.

The limited possibilities of Highbury also provide the background for Emma's flights of fancy. She is bored with the life of her town and tries to find amusement in her imagination. During one shopping trip to town, while Harriet is busy shopping ("tempted by everything, and swayed by half a word") Emma moves to the window to amuse herself:

> Much could not be hoped for from the traffic of even the busiest part of Highbury:—Mr. Perry walking hastily by; Mr. William Cox letting himself in at the office-door; Mr. Cole's carriage horses returning from exercise; or a stray letter-boy on an obstinate mule, were the liveliest objects she could presume to expect; and when her eyes fell only on the butcher with his tray, a tidy old woman traveling homewards from shop with a full basket, two curs quarreling over a dirty bone, and a string of dawdling children round the baker's little bow-window eyeing the ginger bread, she knew she had no reason to complain, and was amused enough; quite enough still to stand at the door. A mind lively and at ease can do with seeing nothing, and can see nothing that does not answer. (p. 213)[†]

[†] Page numbers are taken from the Bantam Classics edition (1981).

Emma's mind is nothing if not lively, and if she finds nothing to amuse her she will create her own amusements. It is no accident that the main thing that occupies Emma's time is "play," for she has no serious business to attend to.

The main thing that disrupts what Tanner calls the "as-ever-ness" of Highbury is marriage, as Mr. Woodhouse is constantly pointing out. Even though the marriages take place within a small circle of acquaintances, they cannot avoid changing things. Miss Taylor's name changes to Mrs. Weston (though Mr. Woodhouse continues to use her maiden name) and she moves out of Hartfield. Harriet Smith's marriage to Robert Martin means that her relationship with Emma changes, and Emma's life will change even though she is willing to live at home until Mr. Woodhouse's death.

As a general scheme, the entire book is framed by marriages. Miss Taylor's comes at the very beginning and Emma's at the end. The crucial turning point in the book is Emma's recognition that she is in love with Knightley and wants him to marry no one but herself. As the book progresses, the attention shifts in turn from one set of lovers or potential lovers to another. Femininely considered, book one (chap. 1–18) focuses on Harriet, book two (chap. 19–36) on Jane, and book three (chap. 37–55) on Emma; masculinely, book one is Elton's, book two Churchill's, and book three Knightley's.

Internally, each book is structured by courtships imagined or real, courtships consummated or undone. Book one begins with Miss Weston's wedding, and the central concern is Emma's efforts to arrange a marriage for Harriet. Elton makes his disastrous proposal to Emma in chapter fifteen and the following chapters are concerned with the aftermath of that proposal (Emma's chagrin, Elton's departure from Highbury). The last chapter of book one (18) focuses on Churchill, anticipating the central male character of book two, and book one closes with Knightley's insightful assessment of Churchill's dithering character.

The initial chapters of book two assemble the characters for the next romantic cycle. Elton returns, married, so book two, like book one, is initiated by a marriage. Jane Fairfax comes on the scene initially and she serves as a foil for Emma. Though similar to Harriet in her origins and social standing, she is superior to Emma in accomplishments. Churchill finally shows up, and his mysterious relationship with Jane hovers over the whole of book two. Meanwhile, Emma and Churchill are also engaged in a quasi-romance. The double romances of Churchill with Emma and Jane come together in the lengthy dinner scene at the end of book two (chap. 34–36). Mrs. Elton is the focus of attention in these chapters, but part of what we learn is that she is trying to arrange for Jane's entry into a governess "trade."

Book three begins with Emma's detachment from Churchill, a romance ended, parallel to her "romance" with Elton that ended book one. The trajectory of this book is clearly to bring the relationship between Knightley and Emma to a happy ending, and Jane and Frank's longer-standing romance is also brought to consummation.

Despise this emphasis on marriage and the disruption it causes, by the end of the story the same set is back together again "as ever." Austen slyly indicates that even Mrs. Elton, an outsider throughout the novel, was not present at Emma's wedding, though that does not keep her from criticizing it: "Mrs. Elton, from the particulars detailed by her husband, thought it all extremely shabby, and very inferior to her own" (p. 445). Jane and Frank are gone by the end of the novel as well. We are back with the "small band of true friends" (p. 446) that started the novel, but the difficulties of their relationships have left us wondering how the band can keep together. With all the strains on relationships and with marriage introduced as a disruptive event, how can these "true friends" continue in fellowship? Are there marriages that do *not* break up the family circle and the wider circle of the community? Essentially, the answer of the novel is that the neighbors can only remain a "band of true friends" by a continual exercise of charity and by continual devotion to truth.

If the constrained and confining social situation is important background, the foreground is occupied by the issue of moral guidance. Guidance is essential if the "small band of true friends" is going to remain "as ever" in true charity. In particular, Emma needs guidance if she is not going to cause continual catastrophe. Her story is largely the story of a search for the right guide, for someone who will speak the truth in love and teach her to do the same. Knightley (*Knight*ley) is the guide here, the savior who delivers Emma from her own folly and at the same time ensures the survival of the community of neighbors in Highbury. From this perspective, *Emma* is a Pygmalion story, the story of a craftsman (Knightley) who fashions a woman and then falls in love with her. It is a *Taming of the Shrew* with a mild-mannered shrew. We see again here Austen's insight that the moral life cannot be lived, or moral character formed, in isolation. It is worked out in community and relationship. We need guides, but only certain sorts of guides will do. Some guides are blind and lead us into the ditch.

Review Questions

1. Describe the conditions of life in Highbury. Why is this important background to the novel?

2. How are the marriages in *Emma* different from those in *Pride and Prejudice*?

3. How do the conditions of Highbury contribute to Emma's character?

4. Explain how marriages structure the novel.

5. Why are love and charity important to the novel?

Book One

Mr. Woodhouse is the embodiment of the "as ever" of Highbury and revels in the sameness:

> His spirits required support. He was a nervous man, easily depressed; fond of everything he was used to, and hating to part with them; hating change of every kind. Matrimony, as the origin of change, was always disagreeable; and he was by no means yet reconciled to his own daughter's marrying, nor could ever

speak of her but with compassion, though it had been entirely a match of affection, when he was now obliged to part with Miss Taylor too. (p. 5)

His "habits of gentle selfishness" may be gentle, but they are indeed selfish. Fearful of everything, he is an elderly child, a point driven home during a later visit to Donwell Abbey, when Mr. Knightley ensures that Mr. Woodhouse will be entertained by giving him free rein to play with the trinkets and baubles from a desk drawer. Mr. Woodhouse is the great man of Highbury; he represents the town's character. But if Mr. Woodhouse represents the town, the town at least is a hypochondriac if not actually sick.

Mr. Woodhouse thinks Emma is a brilliant matchmaker and asks her to stop "breaking up the family circle" by arranging marriages. But Emma's real vices are more fundamental:

The real evils, indeed, of Emma's situation were the power of having rather too much her own way, and a disposition to think a little too well of herself: these were the disadvantages which threatened to alloy her many enjoyments. The danger, however, was at present so unperceived, that they did not by any means rank as misfortunes with her. (p. 3)

From the moment she is introduced, we know that she is in desperate need of guidance, and from the moment we meet her father we know that he will never provide it. She is a sheep terribly in need of a shepherd.

Her lack of guidance has made her an undisciplined student. Mrs. Weston tells Knightley that she means to read with Harriet, but Mr. Knightley knows her too well and is too frank to let the comment pass: "Emma has been meaning to read more ever since she was twelve years old," but she never got further than making neat lists of books to read. In general, "she will never submit to anything requiring industry and patience, and a subjection of the fancy to the understanding" (p. 33). Even when provoked by jealousy for the accomplishments of Jane Fairfax, Emma is not able to muster much determination. After hearing Jane play the piano and sing, "She did most heartily grieve over the idleness of her childhood; and sat down and practiced vigorously an hour and a half" (p. 211). Emma will not work at anything. And she is left to do nothing but play, and play at whatever her heart desires.

What kind of person is qualified to act as Emma's "Pygmalion"? Three qualities are essential. First, a guide must have moral insight, an ability to see reality as it is, to read the clues and symptoms of manners and behavior in order to form a judgment about character and principles. Second, a moral guide must be honest, utterly rejecting flattery and false praise, and be courageous enough to tell the truth regardless of the consequences. Finally, a guide must be humble, recognizing that the person being guided has choices and a character of her own, recognizing the *otherness* of the other. All these qualities can be summarized in a single word: A useful guide must be full of *charity*.

Emma needs such a shepherd, but instead of seeking one, she presumes to be a shepherd herself, taking the naive and impressionable Harriet Smith under her wing, acting as a moral and cultural guide for her. Emma's attempt to shape and train Harriet is comically futile because Emma lacks all the qualities of a proper guide, and above all because she lacks love.

She lacks insight into character and situation for a variety of reasons. For one, she is too full of fancy and imagination. She invents out of thin air a romanticized past for Harriet: The narrator tells us that Harriet is the natural daughter of "somebody," but Emma turns this somebody into a "gentleman's daughter" (p. 27). Later, she takes a few random clues from Jane Fairfax and invents a scandalous relationship with Mr. Dixon, again out of thin air.

Emma's fancifulness is allied to an egotism, for she wants to remake the world according to her own imagination. When Knightley objects after Emma has broken up the relationship of Harriet and Robert Martin and claims that Emma is damaging Harriet by filling her with false hopes, Emma responds by saying a farmer is not good enough for "my intimate friend" (p. 55), as if merely being a friend of Emma raised her social standing. Because her imagination is unchecked by reality, because she is perfectly sure of her opinions, she never sees Harriet for what she is. She cannot even paint her correctly, as Knightley (of course) points out (p. 43). She cannot serve as a moral guide for Harriet because she never acknowledges that Harriet has a moral sense or moral character of her own. Harriet is just an object, a living doll for a bored, lively young woman:

> Harriet certainly was not clever, but she had a sweet, docile, grateful disposition, was totally free from conceit, and only desiring to be guided by any one she looked up to. Her early attachment to herself was very amiable; and her inclination for good company, and power of appreciating what was elegant and clever, showed that there was no want of taste, though strength of understanding must not be expected. Altogether she was quite convinced of Harriet Smith's being exactly the young friend she wanted—exactly the something which her home required. (p. 23)

"Exactly the something" indeed—Emma might as well be looking for new curtains for the drawing room at Hartfield. As noted above, "play" is a key to Emma's character. She enjoys games and is good at them. But sometimes her toys are living people.

Emma is not honest in her guidance of Harriet. When reality bumps up against her imagination, her snobbish pigeonholing of everything, she lies to others and herself. Sometimes the effect is comic. When Elton proposes to her, she assures him that he is mistaken about his own affections: "I am much astonished, Mr. Elton. This to *me*! You forget yourself; you take me for my friend; any message to Miss Smith I shall be happy to deliver" (p. 120). Other times the effect is cruel. This is clearest in the scene where she evaluates Robert Martin's reading habits. He is actually quite widely read for his class and seems to be more systematic than Emma is. According to Emma's preconceived scheme, this cannot be, so Emma simply ignores the truth. Austen manipulates her narrative in such a way that we do not quite feel the horror of this, but Emma very nearly spoils Harriet's best chance for marriage. Emma's lack of honesty is seen even more clearly in her evaluation of Martin's letter of proposal. She is surprised by its quality and the kind of man it reveals, but since again this does not fit her imagination she belittles the letter: It is "so good a letter . . . that I think one of his sisters must have helped him" (p. 46).

Emma is also dishonest in the sense of not being forthright about what she is doing. She refuses to recognize her own failings and feelings. She has planned Harriet's life with Elton and she wants to prevent Harriet from accepting Martin, but she keeps assuring Harriet that she is not giving advice. Even when Knightley discerns that Emma has encouraged Harriet to refuse Robert Martin, she tries to avoid the truth:

> "You saw her answer! You wrote her answer too. Emma, this is your doing. You persuaded her to refuse him."
> "And if I did (which, however, I am far from allowing), I should not feel that I had done wrong." (p. 55)

She is even dishonest and blinded about her own feelings. Later she convinces herself that she likes Frank Churchill more than she does, and only very late in the book does she recognize what has been obvious to readers for many pages—that she is in love with Mr. Knightley.

Emma's failures as a guide for Harriet are not mainly failures of intelligence, for Emma has plenty of intelligence. Instead they are mainly failures of charity. Harriet is the first of several vulnerable, unprotected women in the novel; the others are Miss Bates and Jane Fairfax. Given the uncertainty of their position in society, these women serve as test cases of charity. Despite her intentions and professions, Emma does *not* treat Harriet charitably because she does not treat her honestly. Charity demands that Emma think of Harriet as a great deal more than "exactly the something the house needs." Mr. Knightley provides a sharp contrast: he is indignant that Emma has intervened between Harriet and Robert Martin because he realizes that Robert is Harriet's best hope for happiness. That is to say, he is, as always, concerned for the helpless.

Because Emma wholly lacks qualifications as a moral guide she sows only misery and confusion. She raises Harriet's expectations only to have them dashed, not once but twice. In book one, she deliberately sets out to match Harriet with Elton, and later she inadvertently encourages Harriet's hopes for Knightley. Her machinations are not in Harriet's self-interest and in the second case work against Emma's own interests and her deepest desires. As Tanner puts it, instead of Pygmalion she is like Dr. Frankenstein, and the creature gets beyond the control of her creator.

Emma wants to play Pygmalion but in fact she needs someone to shape her. One of the dominating issues from the first pages is what kind of shepherd she will find. In fact, it is clear that her true shepherd is already right before her, and we wonder how long it will take Emma to notice. Knightley is qualified to serve as a moral guide both by insight and by honesty. His honesty and forthrightness is obvious throughout. From his first appearance, we are told that

> Mr. Knightley . . . was one of the few people who could see faults in Emma Woodhouse, and the only one who ever told her of them; and though this was not particularly agreeable to Emma herself, she knew it would be so much less so to her father, that she would not have him really suspect such a circumstance as her not being thought perfect by everybody. (p. 8)

Knightley's honesty to Emma is all the more important given the flattery with which she is surrounded. Harriet, as Knightley realizes, is the worst kind of friend for Emma; she knows nothing and thinks Emma knows everything, and this can only confirm Emma in her complacency and certainty of her own rightness. This is also one reason Knightley dislikes Churchill. In Knightley's judgment, Churchill lacks resolution and will because he does not visit his father (instead makes lame excuses for it) and he is a flatterer of Emma. Elton is the same, praising where Knightley criticizes. Knightley's honesty and frankness are also manifest is his actions. Unlike Elton and Frank Churchill, who court Emma by manipulating, games, and "finesse," Knightley is an advocate of vigorous and straightforward action.

Austen's contrast of Knightley and Churchill has political and cultural dimensions. Churchill plays games of intrigue, which are characterized as "espionage" at one point. Knightley is not speaking randomly when he says that Churchill has "French" quality to him. Austen wrote *Emma* in 1815 during the latter part of the Napoleonic wars, when threats of French spies and invasions were very real. Knightley, the blunt and clear-eyed gentry landowner is a perfect specimen of English nobility, with an eye and ear out for Continental threats and games. It is on the shoulders of such men as the charitable, knightly Knightley that the future of England rests.

Knightley also has insight into character and situations. He recognizes the clues concerning Jane and Frank Churchill before anyone else does. He is careful to form a judgment and forms it on the basis of reality, rather than projecting his imagination onto people. Still, he is not above changing his mind. He believes initially that Harriet is empty-headed and unworthy of Robert Martin, but later acknowledges that she has admirable qualities. This humility, shown by his willingness to accept new information, makes him a sound judge and guide.

Knightley sees reality as it is but this does not make him unimaginative or coldly rational. Rather, as Tave points out, Knightley has *more* imagination than Emma, since he sees what she is up to even before she does, and he extrapolates the truth from minimal signs and clues. More importantly, Knightley's imagination differs from Emma's in *how* it operates. As Tave explains:

> [His] is not an imagination that creates what it sees, like the poet gazing into the fire, while his fancy soothes him with a waking dream and while his understanding takes repose in innocent vacuity of thought. . . . The effect of Mr. Knightley's imagination is not to make him build a private world of his own feelings but to turn him outward to a delicate understanding of what lies beyond himself, in the feelings of others.

For Knightley, in short, imagination is in the service of truth, not a substitute for truth.

Knightley also makes a suitable moral guide because he does not aspire to control and manipulate people. He is humble about his own contribution to Emma's education, for instance, which is a sharp contrast to Emma's certainty that she can form Harriet to her own image after her own likeness. Especially in the latter portions of the book, Knightley's kindness is highlighted. Though he claims not to have had much effect, Emma does hear him and his rebukes hit home. They become second nature to her, and when we enter into Emma's thoughts we often hear the voice of Knightley. It is striking to read Emma's "internal dialogues" and to realize that she is often dialoguing with Knightley.

In *Emma* as in all her novels, Austen is concerned about the interplay of manners and morals. *Emma* is a comedy largely because people, especially Emma, misconstrue and misinterpret the signals of others. Consistently and comically, she misreads nearly everyone she encounters. She thinks that Elton's flattery is directed toward Harriet, when of course it is directed toward herself. Anyone observing Elton would know that this is the case:

> "You have given Miss Smith all that she required," said [Mr. Elton]: "you have made her graceful and easy. She was a beautiful creature when she came to you; but, in my opinion, the attractions you have added are infinitely superior to what she received from nature."
>
> "I am glad you think I have been useful to her; but Harriet only wanted drawing out, and receiving a few, very few hints. She had all the natural grace of sweetness of temper and artlessness in herself. I have done very little. . . . I have, perhaps, given her a little more decision of character—have taught her to think on points which had not fallen in her way before."
>
> "Exactly so; that is what principally strikes me. So much superadded decision of character! Skilful has been the hand!" (p. 38)

There are a few offhand compliments to Harriet here, but clearly Elton's chief object is to flatter Emma's talent in improving Harriet.

Emma's misreading here is part of a larger and more complete misunderstanding of Elton's character and manners. Initially she considers Elton's manners "superior to Mr. Knightley's or Mr. Weston's" and only later learns just how hard and calculating he is beneath his "gallant" exterior. Her misconception of Elton is repeated in books two–three in her misreading of Frank Churchill.

Behind the comic surface of the novel is a more serious point about the use and misuse of manners. Manners, as noted several times in this book, are a code, a means of communicating one's intentions and desires, especially one's romantic intentions and desires. A man who shows particularly close attention to a woman, whose manner toward her is particularly thoughtful, is signaling his desire to know her better. Austen's basic principle is that one is responsible not only for the manner with which one treats others, but responsible for responses to that manner. Especially in romantic or potentially romantic encounters, it is a moral duty to give encouragement only when encouragement is what you intend. To give encouragement without serious intent is a serious moral problem. It is a double dealing and one version of what Knightley calls the "deeper game."

Emma is guilty of "playing" with the code, giving encouragement without serious intent and encouraging admiration without any intention of returning that attention. She does this with Elton, as John Knightley recognizes. Taking note of Elton's attentions, he warns Emma: "You will do well to consider whether it is so or not, and to regulate your behaviour accordingly. I think your manners to him encouraging." Dishonest as ever, Emma immediately declares it impossible: "You are quite mistaken. Mr. Elton and I are very good friends, and nothing more," and she goes on to privately contemplate the "blunders which often arise from a partial knowledge of circumstances" (pp. 103–4). Again, Emma does not learn her lesson, but repeats the error with Churchill later in the book.

The issue of manners also shades into moral concern when we consider the various men of the book. Manners help to define the novel's ideal of a true gentleman. Mr. Weston is agreeable and universally friendly, a middle-aged Bingley, with perfect manners, always wanting people to come and visit. Yet Emma sees that this does not make a perfect gentleman. There is a "softness" and "gentleness" even a "sentimentality" in Elton's manners that other male characters lack, and his manners are called "gallant" (p. 38), no doubt to be pronounced with a French accent. His speech reflects this; he speaks in a heightened, impassioned way. His constant "exactly so" neatly symbolizes his character. It is more ornate than a simple "Yes"—it is more "gallant." It also reflects Elton's fawning obsequiousness; to say "exactly so" is an act of flattery since it compliments the speaker on saying things "exactly as they should be said."

Knightley, as usual, sees through Elton immediately. Though he does not condemn him, Knightley realizes that his soft manners are only a means of getting what he has rationally determined he wants. Gallant as he may be on the surface, he will act rationally (pp. 60–61). And that means he will act in his own economic self interest. John Knightley also sees it and observes the difference between Elton's manners among men and among women. Elton is eager to please but he pleases so that he can achieve what he wants. He is "playing" with manners as much as Emma or Churchill. His ambitions make him "pushy" in his gallantry. He "pushes" into the carriage to propose to Emma. Later he is shown without the cover of gallantry at the ball when he refuses to dance with Harriet. He has not been able to forgive her and acts out of spite instead of charity.

Different sorts of manners are linked to different approaches to courtship. Here there are two polar alternatives. On the one hand, a match that comes out of honest and open communication between the man and the woman, out of speaking truth, leads to solid and lasting love. And importantly, such a marriage does not break up the larger community but instead confirms and strengthens it. On the other hand, games and charades and tricks are not conducive to love. They only breed suspicion and confusion, threatening to break up both the lovers and the circle of the family and community.

There are two main examples of men who seek a match by trickery and cunning. Elton reveals his intentions by a "charade" or riddle. Emma solves the riddle immediately, and as Harriet "was puzzling over the paper in all the confusion of hope and dullness" she contemplates its closing lines:

> "Very well, Mr. Elton, very well indeed. I have read worse charades. *Courtship*—a very good hint. I give you credit for it. This is feeling your way. This is saying very plainly, 'Pray, Miss Smith, give me leave to pay my addresses to you. Approve my charade and my intentions in the same glance.'
>
> May its approval beam in that soft eye!
>
> Harriet exactly. Soft is the very word for her eye—of all epithets, the justest that could be given.
>
> Thy ready wit the word will soon supply.
>
> Humph—Harriet's ready wit! All the better. A man must be very much in love, indeed, to describe her so." (pp. 66–67)

"Humph" indeed. Emma is so blinded that even this obvious clue to Elton's true intentions passes by her, and instead of challenging her interpretation of things, serve as further evidence to confirm it. The second example of courtship by espionage comes from Churchill, but that plot comes to prominence only in the second book.

At the end of the first book Elton has been exposed as the false lover. To be sure, Emma shares responsibility for the confusion and damage this episode causes, but Elton is not without guilt because he attempts to declare his love indirectly, rather than speaking it in truth forthrightly. Knightley, for sure, would not be caught dead playing a "charade."

Review Questions

1. What kind of man is Mr. Woodhouse? What does that say about Highbury?

2. What is the "real evil" of Emma's condition? What effect has this had on her? How is she an "egotist"?

3. What are the qualities necessary to provide moral guidance?

4. How does Emma show that she lacks these qualities in her dealings with Harriet?

5. How does Mr. Knightley display these qualities?

6. Explain how different characters use or abuse manners.

7. How do a man's manners relate to his approach to courtship?

Thought Questions

1. How old is Knightley? Why is this important to the story?

2. What is the solution to the first "charade" recorded in chapter nine? How is it significant in the story?

3. Examine several of Mr. Elton's speeches. How would you characterize his speech? What does this reveal about him?

4. What kind of man is John Knightley? His wife? What kind of marriage do they have?

5. When Emma evaluates her confusion about Mr. Elton and Harriet, she concludes that Elton was partly responsible. Why? Is this fair to Elton?

Books Two and Three

At the end of book one, Elton, spurned by Emma, leaves Highbury in a huff, and rumors of Frank Churchill's arrival fill the stifled air. At the beginning of book two, Austen reassembles her cast of characters, along with several new faces who will move the action along—Jane Fairfax, Mrs. Elton, and eventually, at long last, Frank Churchill. For a moment, it is not all "as ever" in Highbury.

Austen claimed that she was worried that no readers would like Emma. She had reason for concern, for she had already created a number of other characters who delighted in "directing" others, and each was insufferable: Lady Catherine de Bourgh from *Pride and Prejudice*, Aunt Norris in *Mansfield Park*, and Mrs. Ferrars in *Sense and Sensibility*. Still, readers who despise these domineering women find Emma ditzily delightful. Austen ensures that we sympathize with Emma and wish the best for her partly by telling us the whole story from her perspective. If we had watched Harriet's abortive romance with Elton through Harriet's eyes, we would have felt much more intensely just how manipulative and foolish Emma is. She would have looked for all the world like a young version of Lady Catherine.

Readers retain sympathy for Emma also because Austen provides a foil who is even more obnoxiously manipulative: Mrs. Elton. Pompous and blind, to herself even more than to others, she is charmed with her own insights and sophistication. Like Emma, she fancies herself a perfect guide for a younger woman and decides to take Jane Fairfax under her wing. She fails for the same reasons that Emma fails. Like Emma, Mrs. Elton does not let Jane have any decision or moral weight of her own. When she finds out that Jane has been going to the post office to collect letters, she imposes herself on an unwilling Jane without at all knowing what is going on (Jane is going to collect letters from Frank). Mrs. Elton also encourages her to enter the "governess trade"—trafficking in flesh, as Jane calls it (pp. 274–275).

Mrs. Elton's treatment of Jane provides a counterpart to Emma's "guidance" of Harriet earlier in the novel. Both Emma and Mrs. Elton, in the name of charity, take on responsibility for directing a younger woman, and in both cases the charity is actually a mask for officious meddling. The parallels are strengthened when we take Harriet's and Jane's social standing into consideration. Both are unattached women with very iffy futures, and those futures are not assisted by their "patrons." Emma fails the test of charity in regard to Jane as well. Jane is about to assume duties as a governess, which Austen sharply describes as almost a retreat to the convent: "To retire from all the pleasures of life, of rational intercourse, equal society, peace and hope, to penance and mortification forever." Jane hopes to be saved from this by Frank Churchill, but Emma does not know when they first meet that she has any chance of being saved from this fate. This makes Emma's jealousy and petty antagonism to Jane all the more serious a breach of charity. Just as much as Miss Bates, Jane deserves Emma's care and protection.

One key difference between the relationships of Emma and Harriet and Mrs. Elton and Jane is that Jane has a mind of her own, plans of her own, and a lover already engaged, whereas Harriet is a *tabula rasa* without direction or ideas. While shopping Harriet is "tempted by everything, and swayed by half a word, was always very long at a purchase." Jane, by contrast, can form her own opinions and resist Mrs. Elton's bullying guidance. This again has the effect of making Mrs. Elton's direction all the more galling.

Book two also introduces a second "gallant" to join Mr. Elton, namely, Frank Churchill. Long before he appears, we have a fairly complete exposition of his manners from various angles. Mr. Knightley especially has formed a settled opinion concerning him. Churchill owes it to his father to pay a visit, but he keeps putting it off. This is not an understandable delay, nor merely a breach of proper social etiquette, but reveals his lack of manly strength. A sensible and determined man would find a way to fulfill this obligation, not by finesse and maneuver but by vigorous action. As Knightley says, Frank may be "amiable," but is so "only in French" (p. 137).

When Frank arrives, Emma compares him to the evaluation that Knightley had given. She thinks him very agreeable, but that is because he is a flatterer who gives Emma the attention that she desires and thinks she deserves. The rest of Highbury follows Emma's assessment: "He was judged, throughout the parishes of Donwell and Highbury with great candour; liberal allowances were made for the little excesses of such a handsome young man—one who smiled so often and bowed so well" (p. 188). Only Mr. Knightley is unswayed by smiles and bows and Frenchified manners: "Hum! just the trifling, silly fellow I took him for" (p. 188). Knightley is right: Despite his reputation, Frank operates by principles that are opposite of the moral standard of "truth in love."

With Churchill's arrival comes a vocabulary of deception and concealment: riddle, enigma, conundrum, mystery, equivocation, puzzle, guess, conceal, hypocritical, insidious, suspicious—all the language of French invasion. His games lead to confusion. People think Emma is his favorite and for a time Emma thinks the same.

In playing such a game, Frank risks not only confusing Emma but of deeply hurting her. Instead of being concerned he is amused. He takes no responsibility for the responses his manners arouse. He also endangers the very relationship the tricks are designed to sustain. At Box Hill, his flirting with Emma and her lack of charity in playing along nearly ends his engagement, as Jane becomes disgusted with his games and threatens to leave him. He threatens not only his own romance, but the community as well.

When Emma finds out about the engagement, she is appalled that he could have been so encouraging and free with her when he was already engaged, and in front of his own fiancée (pp. 363–367). Churchill came with "affection and faith engaged, and with manners so *very* disengaged." His manners said he was available and interested, and so he might have led Emma to love him. Manners should be open, and only in that way can they be charitable, truly "mannerly." They should not deliberately send a message that is not true.

Prior to the revelation of Churchill's engagement, however, Emma remains as blissfully blind as ever. As with Elton, Emma misconstrues Churchill's manners. She is certain that Churchill is in love with her, just as she was convinced that Elton was *not* in love with her. For Emma, it is unthinkable that Churchill has any attachment to Jane Fairfax, though Knightley, with more insight into the intricacies of the code of manners, sees a deeper game being played. Knightley sees "symptoms of attachment"—significantly enough as he watches them play a game, he sees "disingenuousness and double dealing" everywhere, recognizes that the letters of the game are "but the vehicles for gallantry and trick," and that they "conceal a deeper game on Frank Churchill's part" (p. 321). Emma sees none of this. She is sure that Frank is attached to her. She does recognize some cooling in later dances, and she also realizes that he agrees too quickly with her when she disagrees with him.

Having misconstrued Churchill, she also acts badly in her relationship with him. At Box Hill she delights in his attention and flattery and flirts with him. This is all the more illegitimate

because she has given up any notions of being actually in love
with him:

> When they all sat down it was better—to her taste a great deal
> better—for Frank Churchill grew talkative and gay, making her
> his first object. Every distinguishing attention that could be paid,
> was paid to her. To amuse her, and be agreeable in her eyes,
> seemed all that he cared for—and Emma, glad to be enlivened,
> not sorry to be flattered, was gay and easy too, and gave him all
> the friendly encouragement, the admission to be gallant, which
> she had ever given in the first and most animating period of their
> acquaintance; but which now, in her own estimation, meant
> nothing, though in the judgment of most people looking on, it
> must have had such an appearance as no English word but flirta-
> tion could very well describe. (p. 337)

What Emma does to Harriet and Mrs. Elton attempts to do
with Jane, Churchill does with both Jane and Emma. He reduces
both women to playthings for his own amusement. No community of charity can be established on such a basis, so long as everyone is only "playing" with manners and affections.

Meanwhile, however, Knightley's moral instruction is leading
Emma on the path to self-knowledge, and also reordering Emma's
preferences and loves. Knightley is not just a teacher of truth, but
a teacher who leads Emma to charity. Knightley's qualifications
for this position arise from his own constant charitableness. As
noted above, the objects of charity are the poor of Highbury, and
especially the unattached and unprotected women of the town.
Miss Bates is the chief among these, the most helpless of all, with
absolutely no prospects of finding a husband or gaining any wealth
or security. Knightley consistently treats the Bateses with kindness. He generously lends his carriage to Miss Bates, a kindness
for which Miss Bates thanks him profusely. He offers to bring
something for the Bateses from Kingston, and we learn that he
has given her apples as well. Over and over, he takes solicitous
care of the Bateses, protecting and providing for the helpless. His
"rescue" of Harriet at the ball shows that he possesses true English
gallantry, in contrast to the false gallantry of Elton and Churchill.

Charity to the Bateses is more closely linked with right judgment, though the point is made very subtly. Because Miss Bates is such a chatterbox, the other characters (and we readers) often have a hard time following her. But if we take the time—if we pay her the compliment of attention—we will find that she is a wealth of information. She provides all the clues necessary for determining the real relationship between Frank and Jane, if only someone were willing to listen. Talking to his father, Frank makes the "blunder" of bringing up the subject of Mr. Perry's carriage. He mistakenly says that his father had informed him, but Mr. Weston knows nothing of it. As they talk, Frank realizes that he learned of Perry's plans from Jane, and he lamely tries to cover up his error by saying he must have dreamed it. Miss Bates is astonished at the coincidence:

> there is no denying that Mr. Frank Churchill might have—I do not mean to say that he did not dream it—I am sure that I have sometimes the oddest dreams in the world—but if I am questioned about it, I must acknowledge that there was such an idea last spring; for Mrs. Perry herself mentioned it to my mother, and the Coles knew of it as well as ourselves—but it was quite a secret, known to nobody else, and only thought of about three days. . . . Jane, don't you remember grandmamma's telling us of it when we got home? (p. 317)

It is clear from this account that Frank *must* have received his information from Jane, but by this time no one is listening to Miss Bates any longer. Austen has played a trick on the other characters by putting crucial information into Miss Bates' mouth, but she has also played a clever game with the reader, who is likely to skip over Miss Bates' blather without attention. She is teaching her readers, as well as her characters, to show genuine charity to Miss Bates.

Churchill "rescued" Harriet from gypsies, but in general he proves singularly lacking in charity. In part, this is revealed in his treatment of Mr. Woodhouse. Mr. Woodhouse has Frank pegged:

"That young man . . . is very thoughtless. Do not tell his father, but that young man is not quite the thing. He has been opening the doors very often this evening, and keeping them open very inconsiderately. He does not think of the draught" (p. 227). Somewhat later, Frank has an exchange with Mr. Woodhouse about using the Crown Inn for a ball:

> "A room at an inn is always damp and dangerous, never properly aired, or fit to be inhabited. If they must dance, they had better dance at the Randalls. He had never been in the room at the Crown in his life—did not know the people who kept it by sight. Oh no—a very bad idea. They would catch worse colds at the Crown than anywhere."
>
> "I was going to observe, sir," said Frank Churchill, "that one of the great recommendations of this change would be the very little danger of anybody's catching cold—so much less danger at the Crown than at the Randalls! Mr. Perry might have reason to regret the alteration, but nobody else could."
>
> "Sir," said Mr. Woodhouse, rather warmly, "you are very much mistaken if you suppose Mr. Perry to be that sort of character." (p. 229)

It takes a lot of provocation to make Mr. Woodhouse speak "warmly," but Churchill's implicit mocking does it. Where Elton is cold and calculating beneath his good manners, Frank is unthinkingly cruel beneath his.

Even when Churchill does a good deed, it has an ulterior motive; it is still double dealing and a deeper game. Churchill does a good deed for Mrs. Bates by fixing her glasses, but Austen signals that his charity is not all it seems by describing him as being "deedily occupied about the spectacles" when Emma comes in. Clearly, this is a pretense, showing that he has charity only when he hopes to gain something from it. In this case, he hopes to spend some time with Jane and so he uses the spectacles as a means to achieve that. Importantly, this is the very scene where Knightley rides by and offers his assistance to Miss Bates, showing a contrast of Frank's manipulative "charity" and Knightley's genuine kindness. Likewise, Churchill's gift of a piano to Jane is part of his game and is offered mysteriously and secretly rather than openly.

Elton also lacks genuine charity. In book one, he meets Emma and Harriet as they are walking to show some charity to a poor family. Though a clergyman, Elton interrupts his charitable mission when he finds he can walk with two pretty girls. Instead of actually *doing* something, they have "a very interesting parley about what could be done and should be done" (p. 82). This is not charity. Though she is not referring to Elton, Emma's words just before Elton's arrival describes him exactly: "empty sympathy."

As we have seen, Emma's initial lack of charity is evident in her general snobbishness, and particularly in her attitude toward the Bateses. We see her several times in their company and her initial visits are quick and formal. She gets them over as soon as she can. She does not show a total lack of charity. She sends a pork hindquarter to the Bateses and, unlike Elton, she actually does visit the poor family. Despite this material generosity, she is not genuinely charitable toward people. She feels uncomfortable with people beneath her. Her snobbishness to Robert Martin is but one example, but her attitude toward the Bateses is the key. She finds it a disagreeable duty because Miss Bates is tiresome, and she might end up having contact with someone even worse. She even does an imitation of Miss Bates, for which Mrs. Weston laughingly rebukes her.

The key shift in attitude, of course, comes after the Box Hill incident, which is the key incident in a number of ways. The "small band of true friends" that goes to Box Hill represents the community of Highbury both in its cohesion and in its divisions. Even before Emma's mockery of Miss Bates, things are not going well:

> Nothing was wanting but to be happy when they got there. Seven miles were traveled in expectation of enjoyment, and everybody had a burst of admiration on first arriving; but in the general amount of the day there was deficiency. There was a languor, a want of spirits, a want of union, which could not be got over. They separated too much into parties. The Eltons walked

together; Mr. Knightley took charge of Miss Bates and Jane; and Emma and Harriet belonged to Frank Churchill. And Mr. Weston tried, in vain, to make them harmonize better. It seemed at first an accidental division, but it never materially varied. Mr. and Mrs. Elton, indeed, showed no unwillingness to mix, and be as agreeable as they could; but during the whole two hours that were spent on the Hill, there seemed a principle of separation between the other parties, too strong for any fine prospects, or cold collation, or any cheerful Mr. Weston, to remove. (pp. 336–337)

When a game is proposed, old tensions immediately come into play. Seething still from Emma's rejection, Elton protests that he cannot play since he is too old a man to entertain a Miss Woodhouse. The party cannot play together, and Mr. Weston's "unmanageable" and indiscriminate good will cannot bring them together.

When they attempt to play together, Emma's boredom and hostility to the Bateses comes out into the open. She shows her true feelings for Miss Bates in an unfeeling witticism at her expense. After the party has broken up, Mr. Knightley rebukes her firmly and reminds her of the Bateses' standing, and of the obligation that Emma has, as the great lady of Highbury, to show kindness to those in their situation. It is one of the most forceful and deeply right speeches in English literature. Emma has just protested that "what is good and what is ridiculous" in Miss Bates "are most unfortunately blended." Knightley concedes as much but will not allow Emma to escape responsibility:

Were she prosperous, I could allow much for the occasional prevalence of the ridiculous over the good. Were she a woman of fortune, I would leave every harmless absurdity to take its change; I would not quarrel with you for any liberties of manner. Were she your equal in situation—but, Emma, consider how far this is from being the case. She is poor; she has sunk from the comforts she was born to; and if she live to old age must probably sink more. Her situation should secure your compassion. It was badly done, indeed! You, whom she had known from an infant, whom she had seen grow up from a period when her notice was an

honour—to have you now, in thoughtless spirits, and the pride
of the moment, laugh at her, humble her—and before her niece,
too—and before others, many of whom (certainly some) would
be entirely guided by your treatment of her. (p. 344)

Knightley's impassioned tone indicates that he has taken Miss
Bates' cause as his own; he is no indifferent bystander. Charity, he
recognizes, imposes particular obligations on those who set standards, on the rich or the wellborn. Just as importantly, the speech
works: Emma goes through a period of deep soul-searching and
self-condemnation, which leads not only to regret but to actual
change, a transformation toward love. Her attitude toward Miss
Bates changes and she pays her an immediate visit. She also begins to show concern for Jane Fairfax, though the latter does not
accept her friendship, jealous as she is of Emma's flirtations with
Churchill.

It is only after this rebuke that Emma can be prepared for marriage—for the proper kind of marriage that does not contribute
to the fracturing of the wider social circle but instead contributes
to its cohesion. Mr. Woodhouse's complaints about marriage early
in the book have raised a set of questions: Can there be a match
that actually promotes the cohesion of the family circle, and of
the community? Or does marriage necessarily "break up the family circle"? What kind of marriages are capable of not breaking up
the family circle? Does marriage mean a turning away from the
larger community, or is it possible for marriage to extend the circle
of charity?

The answer of the book is obviously *yes*, but it is important to
see what kind of romance it is that fulfills this requirement. Above
all, the romance that contributes to the cohesion of the community is an "accidental" rather than an "arranged" romance. When
she comes to recognize her love for Knightley, it comes as a shock,
"with the speed of an arrow" (the wound of love). She has not
been planning this; it comes at her without her asking for or wanting it. Matters of love are best left to fate—to God. Trying to play
God with human affections is cruel and dangerous. True love

always comes as an overwhelming surprise, an act of grace, as a rushing, mighty wind.

Another feature of the ideal match is that it is part of moral development. Elton becomes more irritating and pompous when he returns with his bride. His true character becomes evident, and his marriage has not led to a moral advance but a moral degeneration. For Emma, her growing recognition of her love for Knightley is part of her growing self-awareness and honesty. She does not really fall in love with Knightley, as Elizabeth Bennett does with Darcy. There is not a moment in *Emma* when she is not already in love with him. She thinks of him constantly and is always testing her own judgments and perceptions against his. This is brought out subtly in the scene where Harriet finally abandons the relics of her love for Elton. Emma finds her collection pathetic, but at the same time when she discusses one of the incidents, she remembers exactly where Knightley was standing.

The ball scene (chap. 38) is an important symbol of the kind of match that Emma and Knightley will make. The dance is obviously a communal event. Like a feast, a dance is a picture of a community's life. There is organization and intersection of various people. They are ordered. Each plays a unique part in the dance, but the dance is a social event, greater than the sum of the people involved. At the beginning of the ball, Emma is still very much the foolish young woman she has been. She is a little peeved that Mrs. Elton takes the lead in the dance, so much so that it is "almost enough to make her think of marrying," if remaining unmarried meant that she would no longer be the center of attention in Highbury.

Yet, the chapter indicates something of the future direction that Emma's life will take. Early in the chapter we have a glimpse of Emma's thoughts. Frank is not comfortable being there, and Emma realizes that her attachment to him has cooled. On the other hand, Mr. Elton snubs Harriet, and this is not only a personal snub, but in the context of the ball it is a threat to the good feelings among the dancers. In between is Knightley's genuinely "delicate" and "humane" rescue of Harriet. It is clear that this is as much for Emma as for Harriet. Afterward, Knightley and Emma engage in a conversation whose simplicity belies its passion. There is no need for communication at first except by eyes and countenance.

Knightley's love for Emma does not break up the dance. He does not take Emma off into a corner and he does not operate by tricks and charades. Rather his love for Emma overflows in general charity toward his neighbor. This is the kind of match that will not break up the family circle. It is not a match that encloses upon itself with inside jokes and tricks and games. This is a match whose charity extends even to Frank Churchill, a match that even Mr. Woodhouse can approve of.

Review Questions

1. What techniques does Austen use to ensure that we remain sympathetic to Emma?

2. What kind of woman is Mrs. Elton?

3. What does Emma think of Churchill? What does Knightley think? Account for their different interpretations.

4. What wrong does Emma commit at Box Hill? What is the significance of this event in the larger setting of the novel?

5. Discuss Knightley's rebuke of Emma's behavior, and its role in Emma's development.

6. What makes Knightley's marriage to Emma an ideal match?

Thought Questions

1. What does Miss Bates' speech reveal about her character?

2. What is Jane Fairfax's story? How does that fit into the larger issues of the novel?

3. What do the Westons plan for Emma? How is this an ironic reversal of Emma's situation?

4. What speculations does the gift of a piano to Jane Fairfax provoke?

5. Why does Isabella suspect that Jane and Knightley are moving toward engagement? Why is Emma resistant to this idea?

CHAPTER 7

"Perhaps an Improvement":
Persuasion

Persuasion begins at a point in a romance where most of Jane Austen's novels are winding toward the end. At the end of chapter three, Anne Elliot, who has just heard the name "Wentworth" mentioned, thinks with a sigh "a few months more, and *he*, perhaps may be walking here." "He," the narrator goes on to explain, is Captain Frederick Wentworth of the British Navy whom Anne had met eight years previously (in 1806):

> He was, at that time, a remarkably fine young man, with a great deal of intelligence, spirit, and brilliancy; and Anne an extremely pretty girl, with gentleness, modesty, taste, and feeling. Half the sum of attraction, on either side, might have been enough, for he had nothing to do, and she had hardly anybody to love; but the encounter of such lavish recommendations could not fail. They were gradually acquainted, and when acquainted, rapidly and deeply in love. It would be difficult to say which had seen the highest perfection in the other, or which had been the happiest; she, in receiving his declarations and proposals, or he in having them accepted. (p. 19)[†]

This is far too early in an Austen novel for "declarations and proposals," and the reader familiar with Austen's ways immediately knows that there is more to this story. There is, as she continues:

[†] Page numbers are taken from the Modern Library edition (2001).

Troubles soon arose. Sir Walter [Anne's widowed father], on being applied to, without actually withholding his consent, or saying it should never be, gave it all the negative of great
astonishment, great coldness, great silence, and a professed resolution of doing nothing for his daughter. He thought it a very
degrading alliance; and Lady Russell [a family friend and Anne's
surrogate mother], though with a more tempered and pardon-
able pride, received it as a most unfortunate one. (p. 20)

Plans were called off, the lovers separated—Anne condemned
to life with her indifferent family and Wentworth pursuing success and riches through naval service. Nineteen, impressionable,
and submissive, Anne was *persuaded* to end it.

From the opening chapters, then, we know that *Persuasion* is
the story of an interrupted romance, which we also presume will
be resumed despite the seven years that intervene. It is a story of
second chances. It is clear from the novel's beginning that romances die; the question is whether they can be made alive again.
It is no accident that the first half of the novel is set in autumn, in
dusky November. The question is, Will spring ever come?

With reference to Shakespeare, Peter Saccio has observed that
romantic comedy is about desire, the obstacles to desire, and the
overcoming of those obstacles. The obstacles to the fulfillment of
desire are normally one of two kinds—external or internal. Either
the obstacle comes from outside in the form of some authority (a
father forbids the lovers), a rival lover, or some aspect of the social
and political situation (family rivalry as in *Romeo and Juliet*); or
the obstacle comes from within, such as when one of the two
lovers cannot stand the sight of the other (Beatrice and Benedick
in *Much Ado About Nothing*). If the obstacle is external, the solution is flight; if the obstacle is internal, then the solution is "invasion," the coming of some new factor into the situation that will
break the deadlock.

Persuasion is a romantic comedy that deals with "internal" obstacles to the fulfillment of desire, but these internal obstacles are
of a peculiar kind. The book is not about two people who hate
each other falling in love eventually and comically. It is about two

people who have once loved each other openly, and still love each other secretly, gradually coming to know of one another's love. What stands in the way is not a father, a rival (though there is a rival), or even hostile feelings. The obstacle is desire itself. A *past* love affair makes love in the present unbearably painful and almost unachievable.

In such a situation, neither escape nor invasion is an option. Frederick Wentworth cannot go running off with Anne, because he cannot be sure that Anne is still in love with him. In a sense, there is an "invasion" that creates a new situation—Wentworth comes back from the war—but that invasion does not solve anything, since their past love makes it awkward for them to talk about even such a simple thing as the weather. In such a situation, the solution that Austen hits on is not escape or invasion but indirection. They speak and profess their love, as Wentworth says in his letter at the end, "by such means as are within reach."

As both the title and the background story indicate, it is a story about influence, about persuading and being persuaded, about the good and evil of submission. There are many shifts and changes on this theme. On the one hand, Anne let herself be persuaded to break the earlier engagement with Wentworth, but throughout the book she is firmly persuaded of her love for Wentworth and becomes persuaded of his love for her. Wentworth speaks in favor of firmness and determination but finds through various circumstances that firmness is not always what is necessary, and he himself displays uncertainty at various points in the story. In part, the limits of persuasion depend on what is being persuaded. Anne can be persuaded to end an official engagement, but the heart is much more difficult to persuade out of love once persuaded into love.

The background also accounts for the strange fact that Anne and Frederick rarely speak to one another throughout the book, and when they do very little of their conversation is recorded. (For contrast, consider the number of times Austen records the electric conversations between Elizabeth Bennet and Mr. Darcy.) Anne overhears Wentworth make comments about her to other people, and she studies his conduct, reads his glances, interprets his gestures. But he rarely speaks directly to her and she answers even more rarely. This indirection is psychologically realistic; two people who have been in love have a difficult time becoming "just friends." When they do speak, the conversations are halting and uncomfortable. When they meet unexpectedly in Bath, Wentworth offers to help Anne get home through the rain:

> Captain Wentworth . . . turned again to Anne, and by manner, rather than words, was offering his services to her.
> "I am much obliged to you," was her answer, "but I am not going with them. The carriage would not accommodate so many. I walk; I prefer walking."
> "But it rains."
> "Oh! very little. Nothing that I regard."
> After a moment's pause, he said: "Though I came only yesterday, I have equipped myself properly for Bath already, you see" (pointing to a new umbrella); "I wish you would make use of it, if you are determined to walk; though I think it would be more prudent to let me get you a chair."
> She was very much obliged to him, but declined in all, repeating her conviction that the rain would come to nothing at present . . . . (pp. 127–128)

William Elliot intervenes in their conversation here, and not for the last time. Almost every conversation they have is interrupted—some obstacle (like the weighty Mrs. Musgrove) sits between them. But the greatest obstacle, weightier even than Mrs. Musgrove, is their own past.

The indirect character of their "conversations" is partly a function of their past history, but Austen seems to have a larger point in mind as well. When Wentworth has his first real conversation with Anne before the concert (chap. 20), Anne concludes that he is still in love with her. And she is right. Yet the story moves on for another four chapters and some fifty pages. Whatever could be taking them so long? In Austen's world, it is not enough for the boy to fall in love with the girl and the girl with the boy; they cannot just jump into each other's arms (or into bed) as they can in a modern movie. There is a set of rules in place. Wentworth hesitates to declare his love, and Anne cannot initiate the conversation. They are reduced to communicating through letters and mediators, by means of indirection and eavesdropping.

One effect of this is that Anne's personality seems less bright and lively than it really is. When she does have an extended conversation, she is fully capable of wit, insight, and even a touch of Elizabeth Bennet's irreverence. But this is displayed rarely and never in conversations directly with Wentworth. At the end, the love affair is consummated by Wentworth overhearing Anne's conversation with Captain Harville.

This background story also highlights another key theme of the novel, which has to do with social class, rank, and true nobility. Lady Russell, who is largely responsible for persuading Anne to give up Wentworth, "had a cultivated mind, and was, generally speaking, rational and consistent." Her fault, though, was a prejudice "on the side of ancestry; she had a value for rank and consequence, which blinded her a little to the faults of those who possessed them" (p. 9). Lady Russell's appeal to Anne manifests this prejudice. Captain Wentworth was confident and had a track record of good luck that supported his confidence. But he had no money, no title, and for Lady Russell, his confidence that he would gain wealth and success was a mark against him, adding a "dangerous character" to his lack of a title (p. 20). Persuasion, thus, is not merely personal persuasion and appeal, but points to issues of social ranking and its relation to character and nobility.

Lady Russell is hardly alone in her prejudice for ancestry. As we shall see, the Elliots are far worse in this respect. But alongside the Elliots, who represent old money and title, the novel shows us two other groups that operate according to other values. First, there are the Musgroves, in-laws to Anne's sister Mary, who are comparatively wealthy and genteel but show a warmth of manner and hospitality and a lack of stuffiness that is very much absent in the self-absorbed Elliots. Austen describes the difference between the elder Musgroves, Mary's in-laws, and the younger family: "The

Musgroves, like their houses, were in a state of alteration, perhaps of improvement" (p. 30). She continues:

> The father and mother were in the old English style, and the young people in the new. Mr. and Mrs. Musgrove were a very good sort of people; friendly and hospitable, not much educated, and not at all elegant. Their children had more modern minds and manners. There was a numerous family; but the only two grown up, excepting Charles, were Henrietta and Louisa, young ladies of nineteen and twenty, who had brought from a school at Exeter all the usual stock of accomplishments, and were now, like thousands of other young ladies, living to be fashionable, happy, and merry. Their dress had every advantage, their faces were rather pretty, their spirits extremely good, their manners unembarrassed and pleasant; they were of consequence at home, and favourites abroad. (p. 30)

This is the state of the family "perhaps" improving.

Second, there is the community of naval officers, exemplified especially by the delightful Admiral and Mrs. Croft. Several features of the story push the naval community to prominence. Unusually among Austen's novels, *Persuasion* is precisely dated in 1814, that is, at the end of the Napoleonic wars. Sailors, many of them made wealthy by their service, have returned home, and Wentworth is among them. More important thematically, the sailors are literally responsible for the survival of the rest of English society. It is no accident that the novel ends on this note: Anne "gloried in being a sailor's wife, but she must pay the tax of quick alarm for belonging to that profession which is, if possible, more distinguished in its domestic virtues than in its national importance" (p. 184).

Military societies are ranked by accomplishment and merit rather than by inheritance; a man who shows leadership potential is not denied promotion because his family is common. In *Persuasion*, the military society is brought into close proximity to the ancient landed gentry, and the latter suffer enormously by the comparison. As Tony Tanner points out, the contrast of nobility and naval "hierarchies" is a dramatic challenge to the whole English social system, for the sailors obviously form a society that is not based on "land" at all. By bringing the two societies into contact Austen is raising questions about the true source of rank and nobility—valuable service or inherited title.

Perhaps the central quality that divides the naval community from the older nobility represented by Sir Walter is the issue of vanity. England, as Austen says in her concluding lines, depends for its existence on the self-sacrifice, skill, and labor of the navy. Walter, by contrast, is all vanity. The difference is striking symbolized by a comment from Admiral Croft, who has taken up the occupancy of Kellynch, the Elliots' family home. Admiral Croft tells Anne during a walk in Bath that he has done little to alter the house "besides sending away some of the large looking-glasses from my dressing-room, which was your father's." He goes on:

> "A very good man, and very much the gentleman, I am sure; but I should think, Miss Elliot" (looking with serious reflection), "I should think he must be a rather dressy man for his time of life. Such a number of looking-glasses! oh, Lord! there was no getting away from oneself." (pp. 91–92)

Not getting away from oneself is precisely Walter's intention in having a house full of mirrors. Admiral Croft operates by a different standard; the world is not a place where he can view himself but a place where he can give himself in service. With the naval officers rising in prominence, not only Kellynch but England as a whole "had passed into better hands than its owners" (p. 90). With Elliots moving out and Crofts moving in, "she could not but in conscience feel that they were gone who deserved not to stay" (p. 90).

There is an autumnal quality to *Persuasion* that contrasts with the bright springlike feel of some of the earlier novels. This is partly a product of Austen's decision to concentrate attention on an older heroine (Anne is twenty-seven at the outset of the novel) who has been disappointed in early love. And that focus corresponds to the autumnal quality of the society. English society as organized around the titled nobility is passing away. A different ordering of society is coming into existence. Austen is not nostalgic for the past system, but rather exposes its flaws and foibles with her usual sharpness. One sign of this shift is the mobility of the characters. Emma Woodhouse stayed in virtually one place her entire life and had not even been to Box Hill before the fateful picnic. Anne Elliot, by contrast, begins with her family in Kellynch, travels with friends to Lyme, and ends up in Bath. The mobility of the characters points to the increasing mobility of the society in which they live. This being a novel about second chances, however, perhaps Austen intends to offer some hope for the future of England.

Though the division is obscured in many modern versions, *Persuasion* was originally written in two books. The first ends with Louisa Musgrove's fall and injury at Lyme (chap. 12), a key turning point in the book in several respects as we shall see. Further, Austen originally wrote a quite different ending to the book, one that lacked the famous scene in which Wentworth writes a letter to Anne while overhearing a conversation between her and Captain Harville. Overlapping this original two-part structure, the story falls out in five main sections, the divisions marked by Anne's movements and by changes in sets of characters:

Chapters	Location	Characters
1–4	Kellynch	Elliot family
5–10	Uppercross Cottage And Kellynch	Musgroves; Wentworth
11–12	Lyme	Naval community
13–14	Uppercross Cottage	Musgroves; Lady Russell
15–18	Bath	Elliot family

It is a perfectly suitable itinerary for a novel whose most admirable characters are not landlocked.

Review Questions

1. What is the background to the story of *Persuasion*?

2. How does this background raise the issue of "persuasion" that is in the title?

3. How does the book display an "autumnal" quality?

4. What are the different groups of people in the novel? Which are the most appealing?

5. How does the naval community differ from the upper class people like the Elliots?

6. Why is the book so full of moving about?

Book One

Persuasion opens with a scene of a man, Sir Walter Elliot, reading a book. Not that Sir Walter is a reader; far from it: "for his own amusement, [he] never took up any book but the Baronetage" (p. 3), and rarely looked at any page but that which told of his own family's history. His reading habits are of a piece with the rest of his character, which the narrator summarizes pointedly: "vanity was the beginning and end of Sir Walter Elliot's character: vanity of person and situation" (p. 4). The personal vanity comes from the fact that, even at fifty-four, he remains "a very fine man," while the situational vanity comes from the standing and history of his family.

Sir Walter's vanity extends to his treatment of other people. He treats his eldest daughter, Elizabeth, with extreme deference, who "had succeeded at sixteen to all that was possible of her mother's rights and consequence; and being very handsome, and very like himself, her influence had always been great, and they had gone on together most happily" (p. 5). Mary, too, now married to Charles Musgrove, had thereby acquired "a little artificial importance." It is no accident that Sir Walter's house is filled with mirrors. Everything around him is a mirror—his book, his children—and if anything does not function as a mirror, if it does not flatter his vanity, it is turned aside with indifference. When his lawyer refers to Captain Wentworth's brother as a "gentleman," Sir Walter is initially confused, but then recovers: "You misled me by the term *gentleman.* I thought you were speaking of a man of property: Mr. Wentworth was nobody, I remember; quite unconnected. . . . One wonders how the names of many of our nobility become so common" (p. 18). For Sir Walter, the Baronetcy is the book of life; if you are not in it, you are literally nothing and nobody.

At the beginning of the novel, Sir Walter is in some financial straits and is being forced to consider vacating the ancestral home, Kellynch Hall, in order to save it. Anne makes the prudent proposal that cutting expenses and extravagances would restore Sir Walter's finances without the drastic step of leaving the house, but Sir Walter will hear none of it; he must keep up the appearance of gentlemanliness at whatever cost. He is not keen on renting the property either and makes absurd suggestions to his lawyer, Mr. Shepherd, about restricting the tenants' access to certain parts of the property: "What restrictions I might impose on the use of the pleasure-gardens is another thing. I am not fond of the idea of my shrubberies being always approachable" (p. 14).

Personal and social vanity both come into play in Sir Walter's assessment of the navy. When he is told that Kellynch Hall has been rented to Admiral Croft, a prominent naval officer, Sir Walter is disdainful: "The profession has its utility, but I should be sorry to see any friend of mine belonging to it." Mr. Shepherd is surprised, and Sir Walter explains his objections to the navy:

> I have two strong grounds of objection to it. First, as being the means of bringing persons of obscure birth into undue distinction, and raising men to honours which their fathers and grandfathers never dreamt of; and, secondly, as it cuts up a man's youth and vigour most horribly; a sailor grows old sooner than any other men . . . . One day last spring, in town, I was in company of two men, striking instances of what I am talking of . . . . I was to give place to Lord St. Ives, and a certain Admiral Baldwin, the most deplorable-looking personage you can imagine; his face the colour of mahogany, rough and rugged to the last degree; all lines and wrinkles, nine grey hairs of a side, and nothing but a daub of powder at top. . . . It is a pity they are not knocked on the head at once, before they reach Admiral Baldwin's age. (p. 15)

Naval men do not mirror back his own smooth and untested handsomeness, and they do not reflect well on his station as a baronet. They are therefore entirely disagreeable. Such comments are especially unforgivable given the time period in which the story is set, since Sir Walter's enjoyment of luxury and good looks depends entirely on the success of those mahogany-faced sailors he so despises.

Sir Walter's arrogance is vivid; his hypocrisy is presented more subtly but is no less essential to his character. In the party that moves with him after vacating Kellynch is a "Mrs. Clay," who "had freckles, and a projecting tooth, and a clumsy wrist." Sir Walter complains of her wrist when she is absent but never when she is present, and Elizabeth says that freckles "disgust" her father. She is "altogether well-looking," which is enough for Sir Walter. But the name is significant: Clay is quite literally an earthy name, associated with no greatness or high station. There are certainly no "Clays" in the "book of books," but Sir Walter is willing, for whatever reasons, to have a Mrs. Clay at his table and in his house.

Anne mirrors Sir Walter no more than Captain Baldwin. Though endowed with "an elegance of mind and sweetness of character, which must have placed her high with any people of real understanding" (p. 5), she is ignored by her father and older sister: to them, "she was only Anne" (p. 5). Like Fanny Price, Anne is useful and productive, more so than many of Austen's heroines. While Emma Woodhouse meddles playfully, while Elizabeth Bennet moves from dance to dance with little in between, Anne is called on for every kind of assistance. In this, she is like Fanny Price, but without Fanny's sickliness. When Mary's son falls and dislocates his collar bone, Anne nurses him; when Louisa Musgrove falls and suffers a debilitating concussion, only Anne keeps her wits about her and is able to organize relief. She is competent and active.

At the beginning of the novel, however, Anne suffers from two faults which are more faults of situation than of character. First, as noted in the introduction to this chapter, she had submitted to Lady Russell's instructions and refused to marry Captain

Wentworth. Her tendency to be influenced by others is going to be one of the main issues in the development of the plot.

Second, during the early part of the book, Anne is virtually silent. Again, this is partly a fault of her situation; she has wise things to say, but for Sir Walter and Elizabeth "her word had no weight" (p. 5). Besides, she listens well, and everyone comes to confide in her. Captain Benwick, whom she meets at Lyme, is melancholy following the death of his intended bride, and Anne soothes him and suggests edifying reading. Henrietta Musgrove confides in Anne. At the end, Anne is involved in two climactic scenes in which she listens to another character (Mrs. Smith and Captain Harville). Her position at the margins and her position of supporting others are nicely symbolized by her piano playing. Instead of actually *dancing*, she plays the piano to enable others to dance. Throughout the novel, however, Anne is gradually finding her voice. During the scene at the White Hart with Captain Harville, she has gained enough confidence to disagree with some vigor, and her willingness to speak marks the final turning point in her love affair with Wentworth. At the end, finally, she finds someone for whom her words are weighty.

Captain Wentworth is brought back into her circle through the Crofts, since Mrs. Croft is Captain Wentworth's sister. The Crofts are a wonderful couple, and worth stopping to ponder for a moment. Mr. Shepherd is certainly impressed with them. He describes the Admiral as "a very hale, hearty, well-looking man . . . and quite the gentleman in all his notions and behaviour." And he is, if anything, even more taken with Mrs. Croft: "'A very well-spoken, genteel, shrewd lady, she seemed,' continued he; 'asked more questions about the house, and terms, and taxes than the Admiral himself, and seemed more conversant with business'" (p. 17). She is in every respect a proper sister for the strong-willed, ambitious Captain Wentworth.

The Crofts obviously represent naval values and attitudes. They are competent and shrewd without being mean, well-mannered though unpolished, hospitable and lively rather than formal. But they also represent a different sort of marriage than many that we have seen in Austen's novels. Mrs. Croft is no Mrs. Bennet, nor is she given to "fat sighings" like Mrs. Musgrove. She is a strong and highly skilled woman who has accompanied her husband all around the world, a woman such as Anne might become after years of marriage to Captain Wentworth. And she is fully a partner in marriage to the Admiral. Mr. Shepherd's description indicates this in his observation that she is more "conversant with business" than her husband. Later, there is a charming symbol of the Croft's partnership during a journey away from Winthrop with Anne:

> "My dear Admiral, that post; we shall certainly take that post."
> But by coolly giving the reins a better direction herself they happily passed out of danger; and by once afterwards judiciously putting out her hand they neither fell into a rut, nor ran foul of a dung-cart; and Anne, with some amusement at their style of driving, which she imagined to be no bad representation of the general guidance of their affairs, found herself safely deposited by them at the Cottage. (pp. 66–67)

Such a partnership between Captain Wentworth and Anne is a long way off when they first meet again. Those early meetings are painful. Captain Wentworth says little and seems angry with her. He flirts with both Louisa and Henrietta Musgrove, which Anne recognizes as a dangerous liberty sure to lead to disappointment and pain. From the piano, she watches him dance and make merry, and he only briefly turns in her direction. The most painful cut, however, occurs when she overhears a conversation between Wentworth and Louisa. Hidden from a walking path by a hedge-row, Anne is positioned to hear the conversation (another indication of her passivity at this point in the story), which is concerned with the issue of persuasion. Louisa is recounting an earlier event in which she determinedly pursued her own course, refusing to be "easily persuaded." Wentworth commends her strong-mindedness with warmth:

> Your sister is an amiable creature; but *yours* is the character of decision and firmness, I see. If you value your conduct or happiness, infuse as much of your own spirit into her as you can. But

this, no doubt, you have been always doing. It is the worst evil of too yielding and indecisive a character, that no influence over it can be depended on. You are never sure of a good impression being durable; everyone may sway it. Let those who would be happy be firm. (p. 64)

Wentworth goes on to illustrate his point by picking up a nut and commending its firmness and resiliency. Careful listener that she is, Anne cannot but go away from this conversation "deeply mortified." She recognized her own character in Wentworth's description of a person too easily influenced, and she took from this conversation that Wentworth was showing clear preference for Louisa over both Henrietta and Anne herself.

The visit to Lyme toward the end of book one marks the turning point in the story in several respects. First, it introduces William Elliot, a cousin of Anne's who is destined to be heir of Kellynch and the Elliot family name. Estranged from Sir Walter, William has had no contact with the family for some years, and Anne meets him inadvertently during a walk at Lyme. From this point, William begins to grow in prominence in the story as a rival to Captain Wentworth for Anne's affections.

Second, and more critically for the final outcome of the book, Louisa's fall forces Wentworth to reconsider his comments about submission and determination. Louisa falls from a wall along the beach at Lyme when she insists on jumping down into Wentworth's arms, against Wentworth's reasonings and warnings. She jumps "too precipitously," Wentworth misses her, and she falls "on the pavement on the Lower Cobb, and was taken up lifeless!" (p. 80)

Two things happen in the aftermath of her fall that change the course of the story and begin to offer Anne hopes of a second chance. First, Anne responds to the situation as she had done earlier when her nephew suffered his fall. Her sister Mary (again!) collapses in hysterics, screaming that Louisa is dead, and even the brave Wentworth can do nothing but cry out plaintively "Is there no one to help me?" and then stagger to the wall crying in agony about Louisa's parents (pp. 80–81). Meanwhile, Anne is all business: "Rub her hands, rub her temples; here are salts: take them, take them." Then, "A surgeon," and someone is dispatched to fetch a surgeon. Charles Musgrove, like Wentworth, expects Anne to act: "Anne, Anne. . . what is to be done next? What, in heaven's name is to be done next?" And so on. When everyone is helpless, Anne keeps her wits and responds. That does not go unnoticed by the attentive Wentworth. Soon after, as he travels with Anne to the Musgroves, he asks her advice about the best way to announce the injury. Anne's words are gaining weight; she is becoming a Mrs. Croft to Wentworth, gently tugging the reins to avoid hitting a post.

Second, Louisa's injury was a direct result of her unwillingness to be persuaded. As Anne ponders the incident in the light of the overheard conversation between Wentworth and Louisa, she wonders whether the Captain would not qualify his endorsement of firmness:

> Anne wondered whether it ever occurred to him now, to question the justness of his own previous opinion as to the universal felicity and advantage of firmness of character; and whether it might not strike him that, like all other qualities of the mind, it should have its proportions and limits. She thought it could scarcely escape him to feel that a persuadable temper might sometimes be as much in favour of happiness as a very resolute character. (p. 86)

In the end, we learn that Wentworth was learning precisely this lesson. As one critic has said, this incident exposes the "nuttiness" of Wentworth's earlier views. At the end of book one, however, there was still much to be endured before that insight could be shared openly between them.

Review Questions

1. What kind of person is Sir Walter? What does he do that shows this character?

2. What kind of person is Anne?

3. What are Anne's faults or difficulties at the outset of the novel?

4. Describe the Crofts and their marriage.

5. How does Anne learn about Captain Wentworth's view of her?

6. Why is it important the Anne is constantly listening to people?

7. What happens at Lyme? How is this an important turning point in the book?

Thought Questions

1. Why did Sir Walter remain single? How does this fit into the rest of the story?

2. Who was Richard Musgrove? What happened to him? Does Austen sympathize with those who mourn him?

3. Who is Charles Hayter? What role does he have in the story?

4. Why do Anne and Captain Benwick get along so well? What advice does she give him?

Book Two

In book two, Anne is with her family in Bath. Sir Walter is intent on making his mark in Bath society and is delighted when hoards of people want to make their acquaintance. On a slight pretext of relation, he makes his way into acquaintance with the Dowager Viscountess Dalrymple. Yet he is appalled by the appearance of everyone around him. There are very few well-looking men in Bath and few pretty women. Bath has its pleasures but it fails to be a suitable mirror for Sir Walter's vanity.

Book one ended with Mr. William Elliot beginning to make his way back into the lives of the Walter Elliots, and much of the drama of book two concerns his efforts to do so. With the Walter Elliots established at Camden Place in Bath, William makes overtures that lead to his reconciliation with the family. Anne, ever thoughtful, wonders what he could be up to. William stands to inherit the title and property regardless, and therefore gains no particular advantage in making friends again.

Not only his actions, but William's manners put Anne on guard.

He is the perfect gentleman, polished and genteel in manner, with always just the right thing to say. But she begins to suspect that the polish is really slickness. He gets on *too* well with everyone in the Elliot household, despite their great differences of temperament and interest. A man who is able to ingratiate himself to such a diverse cast of characters must be a social chameleon, who changes color to suit the company. Moreover, Anne senses no passion or feeling behind the appearance of nobility. Like her father, William Elliot is all surface. And, worst of all, he was "not open":

> There was never any burst of feeling, any warmth of indignation or delight, at the evil or good of others. This, to Anne, was a decided imperfection. Her early impressions were incurable. She prized the frank, the open-hearted, the eager character beyond all others. Warmth and enthusiasm did captivate her still. She felt that she could so much more depend upon the sincerity of those who sometimes looked or said a careless or a hasty thing, than of those whose presence of mind never varied, who tongue never slipped. (p. 116)

"Warmth and enthusiasm"—she is clearly still thinking of Wentworth as the standard of true manhood.

William turns out to be far worse, however, than even Anne suspected, something that she learns somewhat accidentally. She discovers that an old school friend, three years older than she, lives in Bath, and she begins to visit her. Anne had heard that her friend had married a Mr. Smith, who was quite well off, but when she visits she finds Mrs. Smith a poor widow, crippled by rheumatic fever. Her husband had dissipated his wealth and left her with little when he died.

Mrs. Smith plays several important thematic and narrative roles in *Persuasion*. First, her poverty, lack of name, and circumstances dramatically set her off from the rest of Anne's circle. When Sir Walter finds out about Anne's visits to Mrs. Smith, he is appalled— both that Anne should deign to be seen in Westgate Buildings, the poor section of Bath where Mrs. Smith lives, and that Anne should make a Mrs. *Smith* her intimate: "A poor widow, barely able to live, between thirty and forty; a mere Mrs. Smith, an every-day Mrs. Smith, of all people and all names in the world, to be the chosen friend of Miss Anne Elliot" (p. 114). Her presence in the novel and Anne's friendship with her highlight the question of the true source of nobility.

Second, she serves as a nice counterpart to Anne herself. Though she does not live in squalor, she is not comfortable or well:

> Her accommodations were limited to a noisy parlour, and a dark bedroom behind, with no possibility of moving from one to the other without assistance, which there was only one servant in the house to afford, and she never quitted the house but to be conveyed into the warm bath. Yet, in spite of all this, Anne had reason to believe that she had moments only of languor and depression to hours of occupation and enjoyment. How could it be? She watched, observed, reflected, and finally determined that this was not a case of fortitude or resignation only. A submissive spirit might be patient, a strong understanding would supply resolution, but here was something more; here was that elasticity of mind, that disposition to be comforted, that power of turning readily from evil to good, and of finding employment which carried her out of herself, which was from nature alone. It was the choicest gift of Heaven; and Anne viewed her friend as one of those instances in which, by a merciful appointment, it seems designed to counterbalance almost every other want. (p. 111)

Anne, too, has had her disappointments, but has responded to them with an "elasticity of mind" that enabled her to be useful and occupied despite her sorrows. Anne, too, had received this choicest gift of Heaven.

Third, Mrs. Smith functions in the narrative to provide the key that turns Anne's suspicions about William into knowledge. Her late husband had been an intimate friend of William's but had been abused badly by him. Mr. Smith's inability to live within means was inspired by William's reckless lifestyle, and when Mr. Smith died, William refused to help. Mrs. Smith also produces letters to show that William holds Sir Walter and the Elliot name in contempt. Once he had made his fortune, however, William determined that he wanted the Elliot title after all, and began to plot to ensure that he would inherit. He reintroduced himself into the family precisely to prevent a marriage between Sir Walter and Mrs. Clay, which might produce a son who would displace William as the heir. William had been paying considerable attentions to Anne, but Anne had already determined that she would refuse any proposals from him. Mrs. Smith's revelations confirm her commitment to avoid William. He leaves the book for London, where Mrs. Clay will join him as his mistress.

William's flirtations with Anne, however, have had a serious effect, especially during the scene at the concert, where Anne first begins to believe that Wentworth may still be in love with her. Before the concert begins, Anne and Wentworth end up next to each other, and Wentworth comments on the recent news of Louisa's engagement to Captain Benwick. Wentworth is not jealous, but he is troubled that Benwick would marry a woman who was not compatible in temperament or taste; Benwick the melancholy poet, the reader of books, was ending up with a lively but shallow young woman. Wentworth's insight into Louisa's character indicates to Anne that he never really loved Louisa, and he as much as admits that he was wrong to flirt with her as he did.

Anne hopes for more conversation with Wentworth, but William continually intervenes to prevent it. The scene ends in frustration for Anne as well as for the reader. Like much of the book, this scene is a commentary on the difficulty of communication between men and women, which was made something more difficult and delicate a matter because of the emphasis on decorum and propriety in Austen's day. Put it this way: It is inappropriate for a man to speak intimately with a woman until there is some structure of commitment; yet, how is there to be any commitment between two people who have never spoken intimately?

Modern courtship has solved this dilemma by dispensing with rules of decorum and expectations of reserve, but that has had damaging effects in the other direction: A young man approaches a young woman and begins immediately to speak to her on the most intimate terms. There is no structure to this relationship, no authority overseeing it. That is a recipe for disaster. As Austen saw, a man who pays too much attention to a woman is awakening desires in her; if he is not in earnest, he is simply playing with her feelings. On the other hand, a more honorable young man may find that he has committed himself without realizing it and find himself required in conscience to marry a woman he does not especially care for. This was Wentworth's near-disaster with Louisa: Everyone believed they were in love, Louisa perhaps included, and Wentworth, honorable and upright, realized too late that he may have to marry her against his desire.

What to do, then? Anne hopes to know Wentworth's desires; Wentworth wants to know if Anne is still in love with him. Yet decorum prevents them from opening this subject directly. The problem is one for the fictional characters, of course; but it is also a problem for the author, and a tricky one. Austen's first solution to this problem involved Anne overhearing a conversation between Admiral Croft and Wentworth from outside a closed door. The Admiral then invited Anne into the room and left her alone with Wentworth so that they could declare their love. Perfectly workmanlike solution that, with the added benefit of connecting this scene with Anne's earlier eavesdropping on Wentworth and Louisa.

But Austen did not leave the climactic scene in this form. Instead she concocted a scene that is one of the most famous in English literature, and which more precisely represents the tensions and difficulties and indirections of love than virtually any scene in literature. Structurally, the second version is the opposite of the original version: Instead of Anne overhearing a conversation of Wentworth's, he overhears *her* conversation with Harville. Both the original and the revised scenes traded on the necessity of indirection; in both cases, lovers send messages to one another through speaking to a third party. Throughout the book, Anne has been overhearing Wentworth's comments about her, reading his glances, his gestures, and observing and evaluating (quite rightly) his conduct. Here, for the first time, she speaks and *Wentworth* overhears. Anne has gained her voice, gained a hearer, communicated with her lover in the only way she can—by speaking to him through a third party.

Anne is in a room at the White Hart with Captain Harville and Captain Wentworth. Harville motions for Anne to come to him at the window and shows her a portrait of Captain Benwick, which was intended for Fanny Harville, who died before her marriage to Benwick. Captain Harville is distraught to learn that he now intends to give this very same portrait to Louisa. He cannot bear to deliver the portrait himself and so has enlisted Wentworth to carry out the task for him. Benwick, he believes, has forgotten Fanny too quickly, something that Fanny would not have done if the roles were reversed: "She would not have forgotten him so soon." Anne agrees: "It would not be the nature of any woman who truly loved."

This leads into a friendly-serious debate about the endurance of love:

> Captain Harville smiled, as much as to say, "Do you claim that for your sex?" and she answered the question, smiling also, "Yes. We certainly do not forget you so soon as you forget us. It is, perhaps, our fate rather than our merit. We cannot help ourselves. We live at home, quiet, confined, and our feelings prey upon us. You are forced on exertion. You have always a profession, pursuits, business of some sort or other, to take you back into the world immediately, and continual occupation and change soon weaken impressions."

Harville appeals to the witness of literature: "All histories are against you—all stories, prose and verse. . . . Songs and proverbs all talk of woman's fickleness. But perhaps, you will say, they were all written by men." Anne takes up the point: "Men have had every advantage of us in telling their own story. Education has been theirs in so much higher a degree; the pen has been in their hands. I will not allow books to prove anything" (pp. 169–70). Between these two portions of the debate, Harville and Anne are interrupted by a sound from Wentworth's writing desk—the sound of a pen falling from his hand! In this story, at least, the pen has been wrested from the hand of a man, and the woman's constancy has been as superlative as any man's.

Anne's rejection of male writing on women's inconstancy is said in jest, but it fixes attention on an important theme in *Persuasion*. The book, after all, is mainly about the indomitable, unchangeable, eternal love of a woman for a man. Wentworth goes through all sorts of emotional gymnastics—he is by turns angry with Anne, attracted to Louisa Musgrove, jealous of William Elliot, until he finally finds his anchor in love for Anne. Anne is fully persuaded from beginning to end that Wentworth is the man, the only man, she could love. She perfectly exemplifies the "privilege" she claims for her own sex—"that of loving longest, when existence or hope is gone." Love that endures when hope is past—this is love by faith, by sheer endurance, by persuasion of things not seen. Wentworth takes up the pen again, and when he does it is to record *his* constancy in love for Anne.

Wentworth is a sea captain; he is no landed gentleman, and the novel does not end with a typical Austen move into a Pemberly or a Donwell Hall. Anne is his shore, the shore that he finally finds, the only shore he needs or wants. Like every shore, she was there all the time, constant, awaiting his return. Organized by real merit and self-sacrifice rather than vanity and pride, the naval community is the wave of England's future. And with it comes the possibility of recognizing, against the pens of men, the persistence of a woman's love. This is the new world that Austen discerns. It marks an alteration. It is, perhaps, an improvement.

Review Questions

1. Why is Anne suspicious of William Elliot?

2. Who is Mrs. Smith? What is her function in the book?

3. What effect do William's flirtations with Anne have on Wentworth?

4. What does Anne learn from her conversation with Wentworth before the concert? How does she learn that?

5. What was the original closing scene of *Persuasion*?

6. What changes did Austen make in the final version?

Thought Questions

1. What is the point of the debate about Captain Benwick in chapter fourteen?

2. What do Anne and Admiral Croft talk about during their walk through Bath? How is that important to the development of the story?

3. How did William Elliot abuse Mr. Smith?

4. How did Wentworth's "own self" stand in the way of an earlier engagement to Anne?

Bibliography

Primary Sources

Austen, Jane. *Emma*. New York: Bantam, 1981.

Austen, Jane. *Love and Freindship and Other Early Works*. New York: Harmony Books, 1981.

Austen, Jane. *Mansfield Park*. London: Penguin, 1985.

Austen, Jane. *Northanger Abbey*. Koln: Konemann, 1999.

Austen, Jane. *Persuasion*. New York: Modern Library, 2001.

Austen, Jane. *Pride and Prejudice*. Donald J. Gray, ed. New York: W. W. Norton.

Austen, Jane. *Sense and Sensibility*. New York: Modern Library, 2001.

Le Faye, Deirdre, ed. *Jane Austen's Letters*. Oxford: Oxford University Press, 1997.

Books and Articles

Berendsen, Marjet. *Reading Character in Jane Austen's* Emma. Aasen, Netherlands: Van Gorcum, 1991.

Bloom, Amy. "Introduction," in Jane Austen, *Persuasion*. New York: Modern Library, 2001.

Bloom, Harold, ed. *Jane Austen: Modern Critical Views*. New York: Chelsea House, 1986.

Brown, Lloyd W. *Bits of Ivory: Narrative Techniques in Jane Austen's Fiction*. Baton Rouge: Louisiana State University Press, 1973.

Brownstein, Rachel M. "*Northanger Abbey, Sense and Sensibility, Pride and Prejudice*," in Edward Copeland and Juliet McMaster, eds., *The Cambridge Companion to Jane Austen.*

Butler, Marilyn. *Jane Austen and the War of Ideas.* Oxford: Clarendon Press, 1975.

Chandler, Alice. "'A Pair of Fine Eyes': Jane Austen's Treatment of Sex," in Harold Bloom, ed., *Jane Austen: Modern Critical Views.*

Copeland, Edward and Juliet McMaster, eds. *The Cambridge Companion to Jane Austen.* Cambridge: Cambridge University Press, 1997.

Duckworth, Alistair M. *The Improvement of the Estate: A Study of Jane Austen's Novels.* Baltimore: Johns Hopkins University Press, 1994.

Gard, Roger. *Jane Austen's Novels: The Art of Clarity.* New Haven: Yale, 1992.

Gates, David. "Introduction," in Jane Austen, *Sense and Sensibility.* New York: Modern Library, 2001.

Halperin, John. *The Life of Jane Austen.* Baltimore: Johns Hopkins University Press, 1996.

Kelly, Gary. "Reading Aloud in *Mansfield Park*," in Harold Bloom, ed., *Jane Austen: Modern Critical Views.*

———. "Religion and Politics," in Edward Copeland and Juliet McMaster, eds., *The Cambridge Companion to Jane Austen.*

Lascelles, Mary. *Jane Austen and Her Art.* Oxford: Oxford University Press, 1939.

Lauber, John. *Jane Austen.* New York: Twayne, 1993.

Moler, Kenneth L. *Pride and Prejudice: A Study in Artistic Economy.* Boston: Twayne, 1989.

Mooneyham, Laura G. *Romance, Language and Education in Jane Austen's Novels.* New York: St. Martin's Press, 1988.

Murdrick, Marvin. *Jane Austen: Irony as Defense and Discovery.* Berkeley: University of California Press, 1968.

Nardin, Jane. *Those Elegant Decorums: The Concept of Propriety in Jane Austen's Novels.* Albany: State University of New York Press, 1973.

Perkins, Moreland. *Reshaping the Sexes in Sense and Sensibility.* Charlottesville: University Press of Virginia, 1998.

Roberts, Warren. *Jane Austen and the French Revolution.* New York: St. Martin's Press, 1979.

Roberts, Ruth. *"Sense and Sensibility,* or Growing Up Dichotomous," in Harold Bloom, ed., *Jane Austen: Modern Critical Views.*

Shields, Carol. *Jane Austen.* Penguin Lives Series. New York: Penguin, 2001.

Tanner, Tony. *Jane Austen.* Cambridge, Massachusetts: Harvard University Press, 1986.

Tave, Stuard M. *Some Words of Jane Austen.* Chicago: University of Chicago Press, 1973.

Troost, Linda and Sayre Greenfield, eds. *Jane Austen in Hollywood.* Lexington: The University Press of Kentucky, 1998.

Watt, Ian, ed. *Jane Austen: A Collection of Critical Essays.* Englewood Cliffs: Prentice-Hall, 1963.

Weinsheimer, Joel. "Chance and the Hierarchy of Marriages in *Pride and Prejudice,*" in Harold Bloom, ed., *Jane Austen: Modern Critical Views.*

Williams, Michael. *Jane Austen: Six Novels and Their Methods.* New York: St. Martin's Press, 1986.

Wilson, Raymond. "Introduction," in Jane Austen, *Northanger Abbey.* London: Macmillan, 1983.

Wiltshire, John. *"Mansfield Park, Emma, Persuasion,"* in Edward Copeland and Juliet McMaster, eds., *The Cambridge Companion to Jane Austen.*

Wood, James. *The Broken Estate: Essays on Literature and Belief.* New York: Random House, 1999.

Wright, Andrew H. *Jane Austen's Novels: A Study in Structure.* Harmondsworth: Penguin, 1962.